Find more of my work at my blog:

www.theauthorstack.com

Find all my work at my website:

www.russellnohelty.com

Bookbub:

https://www.bookbub.com/profile/russell-nohelty

THE SIX-FIGURE AUTHOR STACK

By:
Russell Nohelty

Edited by:
Lily Luchesi

Proofread by:
Katrina Roets

BUILDING THE SYSTEM

In February 2024, I met Lee Savino at the inaugural Future of Publishing Mastermind event. Honestly, I had never heard of her before, but Tawdra asked if we wanted her to speak, and when Tawdra speaks, you say yes.

Saying yes to having her speak was easily one of the best decisions I made in 2024. Also, what rock was I living under to not know Lee's work, both fiction and non-fiction, huh?

People often think we've known each other for years, but the truth is that our podcast, *The Six Figure Author Experiment,* started about a month after we met. We talked for a few minutes, had a meeting, started a podcast, and then I worked on turning one of her books into a comic. It's been a real whirlwind from then to now.

Over the course of the show, we've had a whole lot of meandering conversations, and this is my attempt to condense them into one cohesive formula for direct sales and general authorship success. These chapters are built on a combination of my previous books, plus editing the transcripts of the conversations into something cohesive. It's in talking through all this stuff with Lee and Monica Leonelle (my business partner in Writer MBA), and on stage at hundreds of events, that I was able to whittle this down to a formula that can be expressed in one graphic.

For years, authors have been told that success comes from chasing algorithms, optimizing retailer visibility, and constantly launching new books to keep revenue flowing. But that's not been my experience or the experience of most successful writers I know. A sustainable author career doesn't come from playing a retailer's game and hoping they choose you to promote, it comes from building a system where every book, every sale, and every reader fuels long-term growth.

Through deep dives into direct sales, Kickstarter campaigns, web store optimization, subscriptions, and reader engagement, we've constructed a model around what actually works for authors who want full control over a thriving publishing career. This book isn't about one-time wins. It's about momentum.

What you'll find in this book is a (hopefully) step-by-step framework for creating a profitable, sustainable publishing business that integrates retailers and direct sales into one business. Yes, you can do both, and they can amplify each other.

I'm not here to tell you to abandon Amazon. Retailers have their place, but only if they're used strategically to funnel readers into an ecosystem you control. I'm also not here to tell you that utilizing direct sales is a magic bullet. We don't think there is a magic bullet. Or, to be more precise, we think there are hundreds of magic bullets, but they work differently for each other, and they act differently depending on how they integrate into your specific business.

It requires thoughtful planning, smart automation, and a long-term mindset, but I am here to show you that it works, and that with the right approach, you can build a business that thrives both inside and outside of the traditional publishing models.

If you're ready to take control of your career, maximize your revenue, and build an engaged reader base that continues to grow with every book, let's get started.

THE MULTI-CHANNEL AUTHOR ECOSYSTEM

Most authors reading this probably know nearly every piece of information that I will talk about in this book. They've read the advice. They've attended the webinars. They've listened to the success stories of six- and seven-figure authors who have built sustainable, thriving careers, but they remain stuck, overwhelmed by the sheer number of possibilities, unable to take the first real step toward implementing a direct sales business.

The difference between authors who succeed and those who don't isn't intelligence, creativity, or even having a bigger audience. Honestly, it's not even about whether they **take consistent action**. The most successful authors are working with the right formula.

Most authors don't have a knowledge problem, or even an execution problem. They have a sequencing problem. They are doing step 10 before step 2 before step 6. Instead of amplifying each other, they are negating each other.

By simply doing things in the right order, struggling authors can start succeeding without putting forth any additional effort, and often doing significantly less, because every action builds on each other. That's not **all** that you need, of course, but the right mindset means nothing if you don't have a solid plan. It does help, though.

Lots of authors sabotage themselves because they don't think they can ever be successful, or that making money is antithetical to making good art. They focus on creating but hesitate when it comes to selling, seeing marketing as something separate from the creative process.

Authors who transition from thinking like creatives to thinking like business owners tend to scale faster. They stop seeing book sales as something they "hope for" and start building systems that ensure consistent revenue. They stop depending entirely on retailers and instead own their audience, their pricing, and their distribution. They stop thinking of marketing as a burden and start seeing it as another form of storytelling that invites readers deeper into their world.

When authors tell me that they don't want attention, I ask them a simple question. "Why is your name on the book, then?" If they're writing under a pen name, then I follow it up by asking, "Why is your picture on your website, then?" If they don't have their picture on it, then I ask, "Why do you want people to read it, then? You could have let it die in your head."

Writing, creating art of any type, is an egotistical pursuit. We take weird ideas from our heads and write them down. Then, we kill trees to print books and expect people to not only read it, and not additionally to love it, but also pay us for the privilege, then talk about it with their friends.

It's egotistical as hell and that's okay, but you can't keep these two things in your head at once and expect to do anything but go mad. These two ideals conflict each other nearly completely, and create action paralysis. If you want to make your art, and be an artist, and do nothing but create, then stop trying to get anyone to read it. Maybe people will read it, but you can't expect that to happen.

Meanwhile, if you do want people to read it, then you need to take actions that will make people read it, and bring attention to your work. If you're that first type, then this book isn't for you, and that's okay. If you're the second type, then I'm going to lay out the system that I've found to amplify all your actions so you can do more with less and build the career of your dreams.

RETAIL-ONLY AUTHORS ARE LEAVING MONEY ON THE TABLE

For years, authors have been told that retailers like Amazon are the only viable path to success. And while platforms like Amazon, Kobo, Barnes & Noble, Google Play, and Apple Books offer incredible visibility, they come with one massive limitation. Namely, the author doesn't own the customer relationship.

Retail-only authors are missing out on the higher revenue, deeper engagement, and long-term business stability that comes from selling direct. They rely on Amazon's algorithm to bring them new readers instead of building a system where readers naturally return to them. They lose 30–70% of their revenue to retailer fees, leaving them with lower profit margins per book. And most importantly, they have no control over their sales because at any moment, a change in Amazon's algorithm, a competitor underpricing their books, or a shift in ad costs can tank their revenue.

Authors who rely solely on retailers are leaving money on the table because they're not leveraging the full power of their audience. Selling books isn't about just getting a single sale. It's about maximizing the value of each reader over time.

Direct sales, Kickstarter, and web stores change the equation by turning readers into long-term customers. A reader who buys a $4.99 ebook on Amazon might generate a $2 royalty, but that same reader, if guided into a direct sales funnel, might buy a $40 signed hardcover bundle, a $75 collector's edition, or a $10/month subscription.

The key to making this shift isn't to abandon retailers. It's leveraging retailer traffic to amplify your business instead of relying on it. Instead of treating retailer sales as an endpoint, successful authors use them as a gateway to more profitable direct sales opportunities. In fact, the more you treat them as part of your system, the more they work together to amplify you.

One of the most surprising benefits of building a direct sales business is it actually increases retailer sales rather than cannibalizing them. A well-executed direct sales strategy doesn't just create higher-margin sales, it boosts discoverability and long-term sales across all platforms.

This is called the Spillover Effect, and it's one of the most powerful forces in multi-channel publishing.

When an author runs ads to their direct store, sells premium editions on Kickstarter, and builds an engaged audience through subscriptions, they increase awareness of their books across the board. Readers who see an author's direct sales campaigns often go on to buy their books on Amazon, boosting rankings and visibility.

When she got started, Lee spent **$130,000 in ad spend** to drive traffic to their direct store. The results?

- **$200,000 in direct sales revenue** from their web store.

- **$1,000,000+ in retailer sales** due to increased Amazon visibility.

All that money is good money, yet we're spending too much time siloing it into buckets instead of magnetizing it to you. Direct sales isn't about choosing between retailers and selling direct. It's about creating a system where both amplify each other. When done correctly, selling direct doesn't take away from retailer sales, it drives them higher.

The authors who succeed in direct sales don't see Amazon as the only option. They see it as one piece of a much bigger system. A system that puts them in control, increases their revenue per reader, and creates a sustainable long-term business.

UNDERSTANDING THE MULTI-CHANNEL AUTHOR BUSINESS

A successful author business isn't a simple pump where constant effort yields the same result. Instead, it's a flywheel that gains momentum over time. The more readers discover an author's books, the more opportunities there are to transition those readers into direct customers. The more readers buy direct, the more sustainable and profitable the business becomes.

A pump business is all about direct, linear effort. Imagine you have a hand pump in the backyard: you push the handle, water comes out; stop pushing, water stops flowing. That's what it's like when you rely solely on external sources (like Amazon or Facebook ads) for sales. Every sale requires new effort, new ad spend, new pushes. The moment you turn off the ad campaign or promotion, the flow of income halts.

A flywheel business, however, is built around momentum that grows with each turn. Visualize a giant spinning wheel on an axis. The first turns are tough, but every little push makes it spin faster, and as it gains momentum, it generates its own energy. Eventually, the wheel keeps spinning even if you ease off the pressure. That's how an author business can work when you have a direct relationship with readers.

Each new fan you gain can lead to more newsletter signups, more word-of-mouth referrals, and more sales of your backlist. Those readers become a renewable resource of support and promotion, so your business keeps growing even if you aren't constantly "pushing" as hard.

Translating this to an author career:

1. **Pump Model (Linear):** Focus on retailer platforms alone (Amazon, Kobo, etc.). You market to strangers over and over again, with no accumulation of long-term connections. Advertising stops → Sales stop.
2. **Flywheel Model (Momentum):** Pull readers into your ecosystem—your newsletter, your direct bookstore, your community. Each reader isn't just a one-off sale; they're an ongoing relationship. As more people join, the energy compounds, and the effort needed to keep sales flowing diminishes over time.

The result? Instead of pumping for every single sale, you're spinning a wheel that ultimately powers itself. Over time, this brings more sustainability, greater profit margins, and a stable author career that doesn't vanish the moment you stop paying for an ad.

Most authors start their careers focusing exclusively on **retailer sales**, and honestly there's nothing wrong with that. Lee started in KU because she was pregnant when she launched her first book and literally couldn't do anything else. When authors get more space, maybe they go wide and publish on Kobo, Apple Books, Barnes and Noble, and Google Play, syndicating with PublishDrive and Draft2Digital, hoping the platforms' built-in traffic will bring them consistent sales.

But we believe in being aggressively wide, which means using those platforms *and* being direct to readers. While retailers play an essential role in discoverability, they are only one part of a much larger system. Relying on retailers alone means giving up profit control, customer relationships, and the ability to increase lifetime reader value.

A true multi-channel author business doesn't depend on a single platform. It blends retailers, direct sales, Kickstarter, subscriptions, and other revenue streams into a system where each sale feeds into the next. This approach turns every launch into an opportunity to build momentum instead of starting from scratch every time a book is released.

Instead of thinking about direct sales as a replacement for retailer sales, the most successful authors see it as a way to maximize every reader's value over time. Retailers bring in new readers. Direct sales increase revenue. Subscriptions create stability. Together, these elements form a self-sustaining ecosystem.

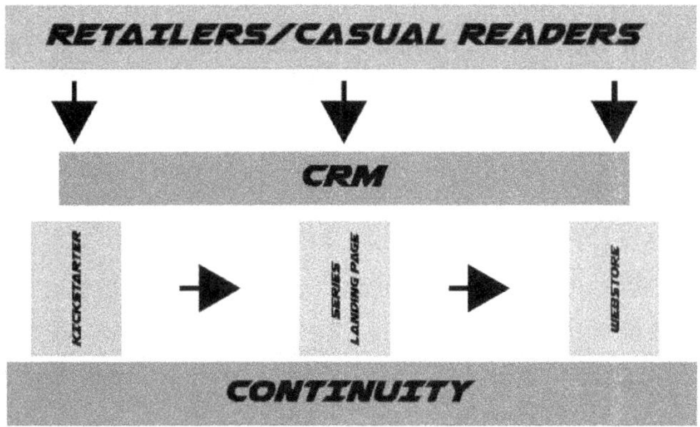

RETAILERS = AUDIENCE GROWTH

Retailers like Amazon, Kobo, Apple Books, Barnes & Noble, and Google Play provide significant visibility and discoverability. Readers browse these platforms daily, searching for their next great read. A well-optimized book, especially one that ranks well in its category, can attract hundreds or even thousands of new readers every month.

However, retailers come with limitations. Profit margins are lower, and competition is fierce. Prices are restricted, and promotions are dictated by the retailer's policies. And perhaps most importantly, the author doesn't own the customer relationship.

A reader who buys a book on Amazon is a customer of Amazon, not the author. The author has no way to follow up with them, no direct way to sell them future books, and no control over whether that reader will see their next release. The retailer's algorithm makes that decision, not the author.

Retailers are great for bringing in new readers, but if those readers stay locked in their ecosystem, the author is forever dependent on retailer-driven visibility. The key to long-term success isn't choosing between retailers and direct sales. It's using retailers as an entry point into a larger business model.

Instead of thinking of a retailer sale as the end goal, successful authors use retailer traffic to funnel readers into their direct ecosystem. A reader who buys an ebook on Amazon might later:

- Visit the author's web store to buy a signed hardcover.
- Join the author's Kickstarter to fund a collector's edition.
- Sign up for a subscription that provides early access to future books.

Retailers are lead generation platforms, not the final destination.

DIRECT SALES = PROFIT CONTROL

The biggest limitation of selling through retailers is that the author doesn't control the customer relationship. That changes with direct sales. When an author sells direct, they:

- **Set their own pricing** without worrying about retailer restrictions.
- **Bundle products in ways that retailers don't allow**, increasing revenue per reader.
- **Collect customer emails**, making it possible to follow up with future offers.
- **Sell premium editions** (signed books, audiobooks, special box sets) that retailers can't provide.

Direct sales put the author in control of the revenue model. Instead of waiting for Amazon to decide how visible a book is, an author can run ads directly to their web store, control the sales funnel, and increase revenue per reader.

But direct sales work best when combined with other revenue channels, not when they replace them entirely.

KICKSTARTER = CASH FLOW & HIGH-MARGIN SALES

Kickstarter has become one of the most powerful tools for direct-selling authors. It's not just about funding books. It's about creating premium product launches that generate high-margin revenue upfront.

Kickstarter has become one of the most powerful tools for direct-selling authors, transforming the way books are launched and funded. It's not just about raising money, it's about creating a high-impact marketing event that builds excitement, attracts dedicated readers, and generates high-margin revenue upfront before a book is even released.

A well-executed Kickstarter campaign provides three key benefits that traditional retail launches can't match. First, it creates significant cash flow early, eliminating financial risk by covering production costs in advance. Instead of investing thousands of dollars into printing, fulfillment, and marketing before knowing if a book will sell, authors can secure funding upfront, allowing them to launch on retailers with confidence.

Second, Kickstarter turns a book launch into an event, generating buzz and excitement in a way that retailer releases often struggle to achieve. A retailer launch is largely passive. Yes, you can influence your network to buy, but you can't guide them through the process. After launch, readers might stumble upon a new release, but unless it's heavily promoted, it can be easy to miss. In contrast, a Kickstarter campaign activates the audience, encouraging participation, discussion, and anticipation for the book's arrival.

Finally, Kickstarter establishes a group of readers who have already shown they are willing to support an author before the book is even printed. These backers are not casual buyers. They are engaged superfans who are far more likely to purchase future books directly, pledge for upcoming campaigns, and spread the word about the author's work.

Many authors assume Kickstarter is only for new or experimental projects, but the reality is, Kickstarter can be used for nearly any type of book launch. Authors have used it to fund:

- **Deluxe hardcover editions** with custom artwork.
- **Boxed sets and collector's editions.**
- **Omnibus collections and special reprints.**

A successful Kickstarter campaign shouldn't end with fulfillment. Great Kickstarter creators seamlessly transition backers into deeper engagement with the author's ecosystem. Kickstarter is not the end of the sales funnel. It's the beginning of a long-term customer relationship. The most successful authors don't just use Kickstarter to fund a book. They use it to build a lifelong audience that supports every future release, engages with their direct sales channels, and becomes the foundation of their publishing business. When integrated into a broader direct sales strategy, Kickstarter becomes more than just a one-time event. It becomes the first step in a thriving, self-sustaining author career.

WEB STORE = EVERGREEN SALES ENGINE

Retailers like Amazon, Kobo, Apple Books, are fantastic for visibility and new audience reach. They help readers discover your work in places they already frequent. Kickstarter expands your audience into direct sales, but it is a limited time engagement, and doesn't give you full customization.

A web store, on the other hand, offers full ownership of the sales process. You set the prices, decide how to package and promote your books, and directly connect with the readers who purchase from you. By owning that customer relationship, you gain the freedom to experiment, bundle, discount, or even raise prices, without worrying about retailer constraints.

Selling direct through your web store means no middleman taking a percentage for listing your book. You keep a larger share of each sale, making it easier to scale income and reinvest profits into future projects. A retailer can change its royalty structure or algorithm overnight, but your own store is insulated from those external shifts. This stability translates into predictable revenue and more control over your cash flow

In short, while retailers and Kickstarter help new readers find you, a well-designed web store is what turns those casual buyers into devoted fans and reliable, long-term customers. You're not just selling books; you're offering an immersive, premium experience that solidifies your brand and paves the way for sustained success.

SUBSCRIPTIONS = RECURRING REVENUE AND LONG-TERM ENGAGEMENT

A subscription model isn't just about making money between book launches. It's about creating an engaged community of superfans who support every release.

When a reader joins a subscription, they aren't only buying books. They're committing to an ongoing relationship with the author. Instead of waiting for the next book launch, subscribers:

- Get early access to new content.
- Receive exclusive stories, novellas, or serialized fiction.
- Are the first to hear about new Kickstarters, special editions, and signed books.

Subscriptions create predictable, recurring income, reducing the pressure to constantly launch new books just to maintain cash flow.

One author built a Patreon-style membership where readers got:

- A new exclusive short story every month.
- A signed hardcover once per quarter.
- Behind-the-scenes content and a private reader group.

Within six months, their subscription revenue was covering all their business expenses, allowing them to write without financial pressure. Subscriptions ensure that authors don't have to start from zero with every new launch. Instead, they always have a base of readers ready to support their next book.

Retailers, Kickstarter, web stores, and subscriptions aren't competing strategies. They are pieces of a larger system that fuels long-term success. Retailers introduce readers. Kickstarter turns them into superfans. Web stores maximize revenue per customer. Subscriptions create stability.

When these channels are connected, every sale leads to the next, building an author business that scales effortlessly over time. In the next section, we'll explore how branding and platform consistency ensure that all of these channels work together seamlessly.

CREATING COHESION ACROSS CHANNELS

A successful author business isn't just about having multiple revenue streams. It's about creating a seamless, recognizable brand across every channel. Whether a reader discovers an author on Amazon, backs their Kickstarter, or visits their web store, the experience should feel consistent.

The mistake many authors make is treating each sales channel as a separate entity, with no unifying message or visual identity. They might have a well-designed Kickstarter page, but their web store feels disconnected. Their retailer books might have a polished look, but their direct sales emails feel like an afterthought. Readers get mixed messages, and instead of becoming long-term customers, they disengage.

Brand consistency isn't just about logos or colors. It's really about ensuring that every touchpoint in the reader's journey reinforces trust, quality, and engagement. When branding is cohesive, readers instinctively recognize the author's work, no matter where they encounter it. And when branding is strong, every new book, campaign, or product release feels like part of a larger experience, rather than just another sales pitch.

The strongest brands in publishing are instantly recognizable. Their covers, typography, messaging, and storytelling feel unified across every format and platform. Direct sales authors can apply the same principles by ensuring that every interaction with their audience reinforces who they are and what they offer.

Authors who don't create a consistent brand experience struggle with:

- Readers not recognizing their books or store when moving between platforms.
- A lack of trust in direct sales channels, because they feel disconnected from the retailer experience.
- Lower conversions on web stores and Kickstarters, because readers aren't sure they're buying from the same author they follow on retailers.

Brand consistency isn't just about aesthetics. It's about building reader trust, so every purchase feels like a natural extension of their engagement with the author.

HOW TO CREATE A SEAMLESS READER EXPERIENCE ACROSS ALL PLATFORMS

The best direct-selling authors think of their brand as a story that unfolds across multiple channels. No matter where a reader encounters them, they should immediately feel like they are stepping into the same world.

This means ensuring that:

- Visual branding remains consistent across all platforms.

- Messaging and tone feel the same, whether it's a retailer book description or a direct sales email.
- Readers always know where to go next, without confusion or friction.

An author's branding should not change from one channel to another. If a reader backs a Kickstarter, then visits the author's web store, the two experiences should feel connected, not like separate businesses. The author's fonts, colors, and overall aesthetic should feel familiar, reinforcing the idea that they are purchasing from the same trusted source.

A reader's journey from discovering an author to becoming a lifelong fan often looks like this:

1. **They find a book on Amazon and buy it.**
2. **They read the backmatter and see a link to a landing page.**
3. **They sign up for an email list and start receiving direct sales offers.**
4. **They back the author's next Kickstarter for an exclusive edition.**
5. **They visit the web store and buy a collector's bundle.**
6. **They join the author's subscription for early access to future books.**

At every step, the branding should feel like a continuous experience, reinforcing the author's identity and making it easy for the reader to stay engaged.

Most authors are trapped in a cycle of constant effort with inconsistent results. Every new book launch feels like starting from scratch. They spend months writing, then scramble to promote, hoping for a surge in retailer sales or a successful ad campaign. If the launch doesn't go well, they move on, hoping the next book will perform better. But this approach is exhausting and unsustainable.

The key to long-term success isn't just selling books. It's building a business where every sale fuels the next, where momentum compounds over time, and where revenue becomes predictable and scalable.

A self-sustaining author business doesn't rely on one big launch or one traffic source. It's structured so readers naturally move through a connected ecosystem, from retailer purchases to direct sales, from Kickstarter campaigns to web store orders, and from one book to the next. Instead of feeling like every new release requires starting over, each book adds to the momentum of what has already been built.

This is the difference between authors who struggle to maintain sales and those who continue growing year after year, regardless of market changes, algorithm shifts, or industry trends.

HOW THE STACK WORKS

In the last chapter, I laid out the elements of the formula, but in this one I'd like to explain how it all integrates together. The publishing landscape has become increasingly complex. Authors today face a constant barrage of "next big things" and "silver bullet" solutions. It's exhausting trying to keep up with every new platform, marketing strategy, and publishing trend.

We talked about this before, but I want to stress that you *probably* don't have an information problem. You have a sequencing problem.

All the information you need already exists, and most of it is probably in your head, swirling around. The real challenge lies in putting it together in a way that works for your specific situation without burning yourself out in the process. What's even better? It's actually simpler to integrate these pieces than most people realize.

Why do so many authors struggle? Because the industry often overcomplicates things. Sometimes this happens because "experts" make money by doing it for you. Other times it's because authors try to do everything at once instead of building systematically.

This methodology comes from over fifteen years of research, testing, and real-world experience. I've experienced both spectacular failures and incredible successes. More importantly, I've learned what works sustainably versus what leads to burnout.

The key is building an integrated publishing ecosystem that:

- Makes the most of every piece of content you create
- Uses your resources efficiently
- Grows steadily without requiring constant attention
- Creates predictable, sustainable income
- Lets you focus on writing rather than constant marketing

Let's explore the five core components of a successful publishing ecosystem and how to implement them in a way that builds on your strengths while protecting your creative energy.

I'm not going to mention a lot of platforms here, because there's not one platform I trust for everything. If you're running ads to your web store, for instance, you probably want to use Shopify. However, if you are going to run ads to a landing page then you probably want something like OptimizePress with heat mapping and session recording for optimization.

Both of those are terrible for running a subscription, which you probably want to do on Substack or Patreon, and you'll likely be using Kickstarter or Indiegogo for running your crowdfunding campaign.

Long story short, there is no singular platform that will save you. That's why we call it an ecosystem, not a platform.

UNDERSTANDING THE FOUNDATION OF YOUR ECOSYSTEM

Before diving into specific tactics, let's talk about the two core principles that make a publishing ecosystem work: leverage and sustainability.

Leverage means doing things once and getting multiple uses from them. Think of it like planting a tree. You do the work once, but that tree keeps producing fruit year after year. In publishing terms, we want our content and marketing efforts to keep working for us long after we create them. This might mean writing content that works across multiple platforms, or creating marketing materials that can support multiple books.

Many authors burn out because they try to do everything at once. They launch a podcast, start a newsletter, run ads, and attempt to be active on every social media platform simultaneously. This approach almost always leads to failure. The smart approach is to start with one thing and make it work well. Only after you've mastered that should you consider adding new elements to your system.

Smart authors think about how to reuse their work before they even start creating. Your blog posts can become book content. Your book content can fuel social media posts. Your marketing copy can work across multiple platforms. Your launch systems can be reused for future books. This isn't about cutting corners. It's about being strategic with your time and energy.

The key to sustainability is understanding that everything you do should be repeatable without burning you out. It needs to be scalable as your audience grows, manageable within your available time, and compatible with your creative process.

Many authors try to copy what works for others ***without considering if it's sustainable for their situation.*** What works for a full-time author with a team might not work for someone writing on the side.

The goal is to build a system that can grow with you over time, not one that requires constant heroic effort to maintain. By focusing on leverage and sustainability from the start, you create a foundation that supports your long-term success as an author. Over time, you can work even fewer hours per week, and make more money, as your system works more and more efficiently.

THE FIVE-STEP INTEGRATED PUBLISHING SYSTEM

Many authors jump straight into publishing without a clear plan. They release a book, try some marketing, and hope for the best. But publishing success isn't about luck. It's about building a systematic approach that works reliably over time. Let's explore the five key steps that create a solid publishing ecosystem.

1. **Continuity through subscriptions** - The foundation of any strong publishing business is predictable, recurring revenue. Think of subscriptions like the undercurrent of your author business. While they take time to build, they provide stability that helps you weather the ups and downs of publishing. You shouldn't obsess over subscriptions when first setting them up, but everything

you do should funnel readers toward becoming subscribers.

2. **Building your casual reader funnel** - Retail sales aren't the end goal. They're a means of customer acquisition. Think of retailer sales as a funnel to convert casual fans into devoted readers. The point is to cast a wide net to find readers and bring them into your ecosystem where you control the customer relationship. You don't need retail sales to turn a huge profit. They just need to work well enough to keep bringing new readers to your door.

3. **Using Kickstarter strategically** - Kickstarter serves as the first step in your publishing journey. It's how you can make the most money from your most ardent backers while creating all your marketing materials for direct sales. Kickstarter comes first because it's a testing ground. You can validate your marketing messages, test different price points, and build excitement before a wider launch.

4. **Creating a series landing page** - Once you've proven your marketing through Kickstarter, you can create series landing pages that use that tested copy. This gives new subscribers a clear path to buy your work. You can create automated sequences offering special deals to new subscribers using the exact email messages that converted best during your campaign. The key is making these landing pages evergreen assets that keep working for you.

5. **Building your web store** - Your web store becomes the final piece, allowing you to sell directly to readers ongoing. While you'll offer all your books, focus on exclusive bundles readers can't get elsewhere. This gives people a reason to buy directly from you rather

than retailers. Remember that once someone buys from you directly, they're much more likely to do so again.

The beauty of this system is that each piece builds on the others. Your Kickstarter creates marketing materials for your landing pages. Your landing pages feed subscribers to your web store. Your web store offers exclusive products to reward your most loyal readers. Everything works together to create a sustainable ecosystem that grows stronger over time

BUILDING THE UNDERCURRENT OF YOUR BUSINESS WITH SUBSCRIPTIONS

Many authors launch their subscription program with grand ambitions. They promise daily content, personal attention, and exclusive access to everything they create. While this enthusiasm is admirable, it often leads to burnout and disappointment when reality sets in.

Instead, subscriptions should grow naturally as part of your overall ecosystem. They aren't meant to be your primary income source when you start. Instead, they're a steady stream that builds over months and years, eventually becoming a reliable foundation for your business. They are the undercurrent of your business, but they don't matter much ***until they matter a lot***.

The key is starting small and sustainable. ***When you first launch a subscription, focus on delivering what you can easily maintain.*** This might mean sharing "burn off" content from your existing work — early drafts, character designs, behind-the-scenes glimpses. Don't create entirely new content streams until you have enough subscribers to justify the extra effort.

Even with 1,100 paying members, almost everything I generate is being used multiple times in multiple ways, without spending a ton of time servicing my membership. Now that we are making $20k/yr on subscriptions, it is now worth it to spend more time working on more community activities.

You don't need to spend tons of time worrying about subscriptions when you first set them up. The goal isn't to create an overnight subscription success. Instead, everything you do should naturally funnel readers toward becoming subscribers over time. This brings more recurring revenue into your business steadily and sustainably.

We use periodic pledge drives to increase subscriptions in bunches, usually 2-4 times per year, and augment them with special discounts that last 24-72 hours. These focused efforts let us boost our numbers and gain attention without constantly pushing subscriptions.

Here is how our membership looked after each big launch in 2024:

- **January 1, 2024** – 324
- **March 1** – 470 (**+*146***)
- **August 1** – 789 (**+*319***)
- **September 15** – 888 (**+*99***)
- **October 31** – 952 (**+*64***)
- **December 10** – 1,052 (**+*100***)
- **January 1, 2025** – 1,150 (**+*98***)

As you can see, the biggest pledge drive was still only 319 members (and it lasted 6 weeks, way too long). Each launch built on the previous one and we welcomed more people into our membership. It takes 1-2 years to build a sustainable membership like this, which is why it's the undercurrent of your publishing ecosystem, not the focus of it.

When starting out, stick to one simple price plan until people are literally begging to pay you more. ***Don't add features or tiers that people aren't actively requesting inside your community.*** Only introduce higher price plans once your base plan is sustainable. When done right, you should see 10-20% of people upgrading over time.

Subscriptions are not the focus of your business, but they are the undercurrent of it. Everything should lead back to the membership, but you shouldn't spend a ton of time executing on it until it is sustainable to do so for you.

THE CASUAL READER FUNNEL

Most authors see retail sales as the end goal. They obsess over Amazon rankings and BookBub features, thinking these metrics define success, but this approach misses the bigger picture. ***Retail sales aren't the destination.*** They're the start of a journey to convert casual readers into devoted fans.

Think of retailer sales as your wide net. Amazon, Barnes & Noble, and other platforms give you access to millions of potential readers. These casual browsers might stumble across your book through algorithms, ads, or recommendations. That first sale is just your foot in the door.

The real magic happens when you turn these casual readers into direct customers. Every retail book should include clear pathways back to your ecosystem. Your back matter needs strong calls to action that guide readers to join your mailing list or visit your website. Once they're in your world, you control the relationship.

This is where most authors get it backward. They worry about making huge profits from retail sales when those platforms should really be customer acquisition channels. Your retail books don't need to generate massive profits. They just need to avoid losing money while bringing new readers into your ecosystem.

The beauty of this approach is it's infinitely scalable. As long as your retail presence stays profitable (*or at least breaks even*), you can keep expanding your reach. Every new reader who discovers you through retailers becomes a potential direct customer.

Anything that increases exposure is good until it sacrifices customer acquisition costs below profitability. You can experiment with pricing, promotions, and marketing as long as you're not losing money to gain readers. The goal is sustainable growth, not quick spikes that drain your resources.

This funnel approach also protects you from platform changes. *When you build your business entirely on retail sales, you're vulnerable to algorithm updates, commission changes, or platform shifts,* but when retailers are just one part of your ecosystem, feeding readers into your direct sales funnel, you maintain control of your business destiny.

The most valuable asset isn't your retail rankings or reviews. It's your direct connection to readers. Every retail sale should be viewed as an opportunity to build that connection, moving casual readers closer to becoming loyal, direct customers.

USING KICKSTARTER AS THE FIRST STEP IN YOUR PUBLISHING JOURNEY

Once you have the base and funnel set up, Kickstarter should be your first step in your publishing journey for most projects.

When used correctly, Kickstarter serves three crucial purposes. First, it lets you make the most money possible from your most ardent supporters. Second, it creates all your marketing materials for future direct sales. Third, and most importantly, it acts as your testing ground for everything that comes after your launch.

Kickstarter is not *just* about raising money. *Every campaign is a marketing laboratory.* We test the copy on our page to make sure it converts before spending money to drive traffic to it. We experiment with email messaging to see what drives the most sales. We track which products and reward tiers resonate most with our audience.

This testing is invaluable. Instead of guessing what will work in your marketing, you get real data from real buyers. Every successful element from your campaign becomes a proven asset you can use in your broader publishing strategy.

We also use Kickstarter to fund production of extra inventory. This lets us take advantage of economies of scale, getting better rates on printing and production. We can then sell this inventory through our direct sales website and in future campaigns. *While the campaign should still be profitable on its own, this extra inventory becomes rocket fuel for future sales.*

A successful Kickstarter campaign should end with three things:

- *All* your production costs paid off,
- A *seed budget* for marketing and advertising, and
- Enough profit for *at least* one reward for yourself.

More than that, you should end with proven marketing materials and a clear understanding of what resonates with your audience. *Everything you build after* - your landing pages, your web store, your email marketing *all grows from what you learn during your campaign*. It's not just about the money raised. It's about creating the bedrock for your entire publishing ecosystem.

This is why timing matters so much. Running a Kickstarter too late in your publishing journey means missing out on all this valuable testing and foundation building. Start with Kickstarter, learn from your campaign, then use those insights to build everything else.

CONVERTING SUCCESS INTO LASTING ASSETS THROUGH LANDING PAGES

Once your Kickstarter wraps and you've proven your marketing copy works, it's time to turn that success into something permanent. This is where series landing pages come into play. They're not just web pages. They're conversion machines built on proven messaging.

We create a series landing page using **the exact copy** we tested in our Kickstarter. No guessing, no reinventing the wheel. We know this messaging works because we've already seen it convert real buyers, but now, instead of a time-limited campaign, we're building an evergreen asset that keeps working for us.

We're using a landing page instead of a web store because we know our Kickstarter page works, and we want to replicate that success as easily as possible.

Once the page is set up, we create a sequence to present new subscribers with a "special offer" for our series at a healthy discount. This sequence uses **the exact email messages** that converted best during our Kickstarter campaign. Again, we're not guessing. We're using proven winners.

This becomes your reader's first introduction to your direct sales environment. You're training them to buy directly from you instead of retailers. Our offers use evergreen countdown timers so everyone who hits the site starts at the same place, no matter when they join, and we consider that initial discount an investment in our relationship with them.

It's important to note here that we **never** offer this exact discount again. This first discount should be the absolute best deal anyone can ever get on your series. When you stick to this rule, it creates real urgency and rewards people for taking quick action. If readers know they can always get the same deal later, they have no reason to act now.

We use heat mapping and session recording to test these pages with new readers. This lets us make small improvements over time that increase conversion rates. Once we have a template that works well, we can create additional special offers periodically with limited-time deals.

The beauty of this approach is that ***until this point, we haven't spent a dollar on advertising***. We're building our foundation on organic reach and proven messaging. Only after we know our funnel works do we consider adding paid traffic to accelerate growth.

ADDING IN YOUR WEB STORE STRATEGY

Your web store isn't just another sales channel. It's the final piece of your integrated publishing ecosystem. It's the place where all your previous efforts converge to create direct relationships with readers.

After creating landing pages and testing your marketing through Kickstarter, your web store becomes the mechanism for ongoing direct sales. The goal isn't to compete with retailers, ***especially since they are funneling casual readers to you***, but to create an exclusive experience that gives readers a compelling reason to buy directly from you.

While you'll offer all your books, ***the focus should be on creating exclusive bundles readers can't find elsewhere.*** This approach gives people a unique reason to visit your site and purchase directly from you.

The most important metric? ***Repeat purchases***. Once somebody buys from you, they become open to buying from you again. This is the entire game of direct sales.

Create a strategic approach to discounts that make each purchase feel like a special opportunity. Make sure to segment customers who purchase through your web store so they don't get your ***even better*** offer.

Your web store isn't an isolated channel. It's the final step in a carefully constructed publishing ecosystem. Your Kickstarter creates marketing materials. Your landing pages feed subscribers. Your web store offers exclusive products that reward your most loyal readers. Everything works together to create a sustainable ecosystem that grows stronger with each sale.

This approach is all about simplicity. You're not just selling books. You're building a direct relationship with readers, one exclusive bundle at a time. And in a world of increasingly complex publishing strategies, sometimes the simplest approach is the most powerful.

THE ADVANCED SET

Advanced optimization isn't about doing more. ***It's about doing the right things strategically and efficiently***. Most authors chase every marketing tactic, burning themselves out in the process, but true optimization is about understanding where your energy creates the most impact.

Advertising enters the ecosystem only after you've tested and proven your foundational elements. Running ads before your funnel is optimized is like pouring water into a leaky bucket. You'll waste resources without seeing meaningful returns.

When you're ready to add advertising, focus on your best bundle offer or series landing page. The goal isn't immediate massive sales, but creating a sustainable pathway for reader acquisition.

The key is testing. Not endless, exhausting testing, but strategic experiments that provide clear insights. Track your metrics carefully. Understand which elements of your funnel convert most effectively. A small, targeted ad spend can generate spillover sales across multiple platforms, potentially reaching six-figure results when done correctly.

Optimization isn't about maximizing every single metric. It's about creating a system that generates predictable, sustainable income while protecting your creative energy.

The Joy of Missing Out (JOMO) isn't just a cute phrase. It's a strategic approach to building your author business. Many authors leave money on the table by trying to optimize everything. Instead, focus on the 20% of activities that generate 80% of your results. Your time and creative energy are your most valuable resources. Protect them fiercely.

This doesn't mean being lazy. It means being intentional. Choose the platforms and strategies that align naturally with your strengths. Build systems that work even when you're not actively pushing them. Create an ecosystem that grows with minimal constant intervention.

The most successful authors aren't those who work the hardest. They're those who work the smartest. They build repeatable processes. They create content that serves multiple purposes. They understand that true optimization is about working in harmony with your natural strengths, not fighting against them.

Remember, your goal isn't to become a marketing machine. Your goal is to create a sustainable publishing business that supports your writing, not consumes it. Advanced optimization is about finding that delicate balance—

generating enough income to support your creative work while maintaining the freedom and autonomy that drew you to writing in the first place.

BRINGING IT ALL TOGETHER

The publishing world *loves* to overcomplicate things. Authors are bombarded with endless strategies, platforms, and "revolutionary" marketing techniques. But direct sales isn't about chasing every shiny new opportunity. It's about creating a systematic approach that works reliably and grows with you.

Direct sales isn't just selling books outside traditional retail channels. It's about building a direct relationship with your readers. Every sale is an opportunity to transform a casual reader into a loyal fan. This means thinking beyond individual transactions and focusing on creating an entire ecosystem around your work.

Your direct sales strategy should integrate multiple channels—Kickstarter, landing pages, web stores, subscriptions—each working together to create a seamless reader experience. The goal isn't to replace retailers but to create additional pathways for readers to discover and engage with your work.

Platforms like Kickstarter become more than just funding mechanisms. They're testing grounds for marketing messages, ways to validate audience interest, and opportunities to build excitement before a wider launch. Your landing pages transform from static web pages into conversion machines, using proven messaging from your most successful campaigns.

Most authors approach their writing as a creative pursuit, separating it completely from business strategy, but the most successful authors understand that creativity and business are deeply interconnected. ***Your publishing ecosystem isn't just about selling books. It's about creating a sustainable business that supports your creative vision.***

This means thinking strategically about every piece of content you create. How can one piece of work serve multiple purposes? A blog post might become a book chapter. A character sketch could become newsletter content. A Kickstarter campaign becomes a marketing laboratory for future projects.

The key is leverage. Do the work once, but create multiple pathways for that work to generate value. This isn't about working harder. It's about working smarter. It's about building systems that continue generating value long after the initial creative effort.

Sustainability isn't a buzzword; it's a strategic approach to protecting your creative energy. Many authors burn out trying to be everywhere, do everything, chase every trend. But the most successful authors are selective. They understand their strengths and build systems that amplify those strengths.

Your author business should feel like an ecosystem; interconnected, adaptable, and capable of growth with minimal constant intervention. It should support your writing, not consume it. Each element should work together, creating a whole that's greater than the sum of its parts.

This approach requires a mindset shift. Stop thinking like a struggling artist hoping for a big break. Start thinking like a creative entrepreneur building a sustainable business. Your writing is your product. Your ecosystem is your business strategy.

The most powerful publishing strategy isn't about finding the perfect marketing hack. It's about creating a system that works for you, protects your creative energy, and grows steadily over time. It's about building an author business that feels less like constant hustle and more like a natural extension of your creative work.

UNDERSTANDING PSYCHOLOGICAL TRIGGERS IN BOOK MARKETING

We've now built the elements of your system, but we need to speak to the undercurrents that help make the system amplify on each other. For years, authors have done little more than shout "buy my book" when they launch their newest project. You've likely seen these messages flooding social media feeds, author newsletters, and book events. While the enthusiasm is admirable, this direct approach often falls flat, leaving authors frustrated and readers unmoved.

Plus, it doesn't work. Or, that is to say, it won't work with anyone who isn't already a diehard fan of your work. So, we have a method that doesn't work ***and*** makes everyone feel uncomfortable. Is there any wonder why writers hate marketing?

When I coach an author, we start with a different premise and try to build something *fun* for everyone involved. I know you're thinking, "Fun and book marketing together? That's impossible."

And it is…if you follow the "traditional" playbook, but we're using a different playbook today because I am 100% certain that marketing can be fun for ***both you and your readers***.

I will also bet dollars to donuts that by the end of this, you'll find something you think is fun, too. ***The challenge lies not in the desire to sell, but in the methodology.***

This is where psychological triggers enter the picture. These subtle yet powerful tools tap into the natural ways humans make decisions and form connections. Rather than creating resistance through direct pressure, *psychological triggers work with our innate decision-making processes, making the path to purchase feel natural and self-directed.*

To understand how this works, consider how you made your last significant purchase. Perhaps you bought a new phone or chose a vacation destination. The decision likely wasn't made because someone simply told you to buy it. Instead, you probably went through a journey of discovery, evaluation, and emotional connection before making your choice. This same principle applies to book sales and reader relationships.

The key difference between traditional direct sales and trigger-based approaches lies in the depth of connection. While traditional methods focus on *the transaction*, psychological triggers build *relationships*. They create a foundation of trust and understanding that makes readers not just willing to buy, but eager to support an author's work.

This shift in approach requires understanding five crucial types of psychological triggers that influence human decision-making. Each trigger serves a specific purpose in building authentic connections with readers, and when used together, they create a comprehensive framework for meaningful author-reader relationships.

BUILDING MEANINGFUL CONNECTIONS

At its heart, successful book marketing isn't about transactions. ***It's about building a community of engaged readers who genuinely care about your work.*** Think of it like cultivating a garden rather than running a vending machine. Just as a garden requires patience, attention, and understanding of natural growth patterns, building reader relationships demands genuine care and strategic nurturing.

When we shift our focus from immediate sales to long-term relationships, something remarkable happens. ***Readers transform from passive consumers into active participants in your author journey.*** They become invested not just in your current book, but in your entire creative process. This is the difference between having customers and building a fandom.

Consider how the most successful authors engage with their readers. They don't just announce book releases - they share their creative process, discuss their inspirations, and create spaces for readers to connect with both the author and each other. This approach builds what marketers call "reader loyalty," but what I prefer to think of as "reader partnership."

The magic happens when you start viewing your readers as collaborators in your author journey rather than just buyers of your product. When readers feel this level of connection, they naturally want to support your work. They become advocates who eagerly await your next release and enthusiastically recommend your books to others. This organic word-of-mouth marketing is far more powerful than any number of "buy my book" posts could ever be.

But how do we create these deeper connections? It starts with understanding that every reader interaction is an opportunity to strengthen your relationship with your audience. Whether it's through your newsletter, social media posts, or in-person events, each touchpoint should add value to your readers' experience beyond just promoting your books.

Think about your favorite authors or creators. What makes you excited to support their work? Is it just the quality of their content, or is it the way they make you feel part of something larger? This same principle applies to your own marketing efforts. When you focus on creating meaningful experiences for your readers, the sales often take care of themselves.

The key is authenticity. Readers can sense when an author is genuinely interested in building a community versus simply making sales. This authenticity, combined with strategic use of psychological triggers, creates a marketing approach that feels natural and enjoyable for both authors and readers.

We're about to explore the specific psychological triggers that make this approach work, but remember: ***the foundation of all successful book marketing is genuine connection.*** Without this foundation, even the most sophisticated marketing techniques will fall flat. With it, you'll find that marketing becomes less about selling and more about sharing your passion with people who are genuinely excited to be part of your author journey.

WHY TRADITIONAL MARKETING FALLS SHORT

Let's talk about a fundamental flaw in how retailers have trained authors to think about book marketing. The traditional approach focuses entirely on what we call "the easy yes"; *those readers who are already primed to buy your book with minimal persuasion*. You know the type: they've read all your previous works, they follow you on social media, they're eagerly awaiting your next release.

These are the people who love a specific genre and know exactly what they want. They will "one-click buy" your book from cover alone.

Retailers *love* these easy yeses because they're efficient. *About one in five people might be an easy yes, and traditional marketing is designed to capture these low-hanging fruit.* It's why Amazon's algorithms focus on showing books to people who've bought similar titles, or why bookstores display new releases by established authors front and center. The system is built to funnel warm leads toward quick sales.

But here's the problem: *focusing solely on easy yeses means you're ignoring 80% of your potential audience.* These are readers who might love your book but need more than a simple "buy now" button to be convinced. They require a different approach, a more sophisticated marketing strategy that builds a compelling case for your work.

Even if someone enjoys romance novels, they might not immediately buy your romance book just because it exists.

Maybe they're overwhelmed with their current reading list, or they're hesitant to try a new author, or they're not sure if your particular take on romance will resonate with them. These aren't easy yeses, but they could become enthusiastic readers if approached correctly.

This is where psychological triggers enter the picture. Instead of focusing on the quick sale, we use a combination of powerful strategies first identified by Monica Leonelle to create multiple pathways to purchase. There are:

- *Core Wounds*
- *Pleasure and Pain Inducers*
- *X-Factors*
- *Connection Deepeners*
- *Button-Pushers*

Each trigger addresses different aspects of the reader's decision-making process, allowing us to connect with potential readers who need more than just awareness to make a purchase.

The more different ways you share about something, the more chances you have to sell to somebody. One reader might connect with your personal story (X-Factor), while another responds to how you address their deeply held fears (Core Wounds). Someone else might be drawn in by the community you've built (Connection Deepeners), while others are motivated by the transformation you promise (Pleasure and Pain Inducers).

By moving beyond the easy yes, you're not just expanding your potential audience, you're building a more sustainable author platform. You're creating deeper connections that lead to long-term readers rather than one-time buyers. This approach takes more time and effort than traditional marketing, but it results in something far more valuable: a dedicated readership that grows organically over time.

The retailers won't teach you this because it doesn't serve their immediate needs. They want quick sales and easy metrics. As an author, your goals should be bigger. You're not just selling books, you're building a career, creating a community, and making a lasting impact on your readers' lives.

UNDERSTANDING CORE WOUNDS

When we talk about core wounds in marketing, we're exploring something far deeper than simple pain points or customer needs. These are the fundamental emotional injuries that shape how people view themselves and interact with the world. Think of them as the deep grooves in our psychological landscape, carved by experiences often dating back to childhood.

Core wounds manifest in six primary transformational paths, each representing a journey from pain to healing:

- **Rejection to Acceptance:** This wound centers on the deep human need to belong. People carrying this wound constantly seek validation, afraid they'll never truly fit in. Your marketing might speak to how your work helps readers find their tribe or validates their experiences.
- **Control to Surrender:** Here we find people struggling with uncertainty and chaos. They grip tightly to whatever they can control, often missing the beauty of letting go. Your content could explore how embracing uncertainty leads to unexpected gifts.
- **Abandonment to Integration:** This wound touches on our fear of being left behind or forgotten. Those

carrying this wound often struggle to trust or form deep connections. Your messaging might focus on building lasting relationships and creating stable foundations.

- **Shame to Honor:** Perhaps one of the most profound wounds, shame makes people feel inherently flawed or unworthy. Your marketing could demonstrate pathways to self-acceptance and pride in one's authentic self.
- **Betrayal to Devotion:** This wound impacts how people trust and form relationships. Those carrying it often expect to be let down or deceived. Your content might explore themes of loyalty, trust-building, and genuine connection.
- **Injustice to Equality:** This wound stems from experiences of unfairness or discrimination. People carrying it are highly attuned to power imbalances and seek level playing fields. Your marketing could address how your work contributes to fairness and equal opportunity.

The power of understanding these core wounds lies in how we use them. It's not about exploiting pain points, but about creating genuine paths to healing. When you structure your marketing around addressing these wounds, you're not just selling a product; you're offering transformation.

If you're writing a fantasy novel about an outcast who finds their place in the world, you're speaking directly to the rejection-to-acceptance wound. Your marketing shouldn't just promote the book's plot. It should emphasize how the story helps readers process their own feelings of exclusion and find their path to belonging.

The key is authenticity. ***Readers can sense when you're genuinely addressing their deep emotional needs versus simply using their pain to make a sale.*** This is why the most effective marketing often comes from authors who have worked through these same wounds themselves. They can speak to both the pain and the possibility of healing from a place of genuine understanding.

What makes core wounds such a powerful foundation for marketing is their universality. While we might experience them differently, these fundamental hurts are part of the human experience. By acknowledging and addressing them respectfully, we create marketing that resonates on a profound level, making readers feel truly seen and understood.

The goal isn't to fix these wounds. That's beyond the scope of what we do as marketers. Instead, we're creating safe spaces where these wounds can be acknowledged, understood, and gently tended. This approach transforms marketing from a transaction into a healing journey that benefits both author and reader.

PLEASURE AND PAIN INDUCERS

At our core, humans experience the world through two fundamental lenses: pleasure and pain. These emotional experiences drive our decision-making in profound and often unconscious ways. Understanding how to work with these emotional drivers can transform your marketing from mere promotion to meaningful engagement.

We might consider ourselves "logical creatures," but emotions drive decisions, while logic justifies them after the fact. You can come up with rational reasons to justify any decision, but the initial impulse was purely emotional. This is how the human brain works; ***emotion leads and logic follows.***

In marketing, pleasure and pain inducers serve as emotional resonance points. They help readers connect with your work on a visceral level. A romance novel doesn't just tell a love story. It taps into the pleasure of falling in love and the pain of loneliness. A thriller doesn't just offer suspense. It plays with the pleasure of solving mysteries and the pain of uncertainty.

The key is to understand that these emotional triggers aren't meant to manipulate - they're meant to create authentic connections. ***When you share your own experiences with pleasure and pain in your marketing, you're inviting readers into a shared emotional space.*** You're saying, "I understand what you're feeling because I've felt it too."

Consider how this works in practice. Let's say you're marketing a self-help book about personal growth. Instead of just listing its features ("10 chapters of actionable advice!"), you might tap into:

The pain points:

- The frustration of feeling stuck
- The exhaustion of trying and failing
- The fear of never reaching your potential

And balance them with pleasure points:

- The joy of breakthrough moments
- The satisfaction of personal progress
- The excitement of discovering new possibilities

It's a balance, and they work best in parity with each other. You can't focus too heavily on pain points by creating marketing that feels heavy and depressing, or lean too far into pleasure, making promises that feel unrealistic. The magic lies in acknowledging the pain while illuminating the path to pleasure.

Your marketing should create what I call an "emotional arc." Start by showing readers you understand their current emotional state (*often pain-based*). Then, guide them through the possibility of transformation, painting a vivid picture of what could be (*pleasure-based*). Finally, position your work as the bridge between these two states.

This approach works because it mirrors how we naturally process emotional experiences. Most of the time, we don't jump directly from pain to pleasure. We need to feel understood in our current state before we're ready to envision change. Your marketing should honor this journey, creating space for both the current reality and the potential future.

One powerful technique is to develop what I call "emotional echoes" in your marketing. These are recurring themes or phrases that resonate with both the pain and pleasure aspects of your readers' experiences. For example, "From overwhelmed to overjoyed" or "Transform your struggle into strength." These paired concepts create emotional bookends that readers can relate to.

Remember, *every reader is on their own emotional journey.* Your job isn't to force them into feeling certain emotions, but to create marketing that recognizes and respects where they are while gently illuminating where they could be. This approach builds trust and creates deeper connections than traditional feature-focused marketing ever could.

By unlocking more pain and pleasure inducers in your marketing, you can give permission for more people to read your work. Maybe one pain inducer is clear from your cover and blurb, but if you embed several more into your work, and unearth them through your marketing, you can exponentially increase your market.

X-FACTOR

In today's market, being good at writing is often not enough anymore. The market is flooded with talented authors, all vying for reader attention. This is where the X-Factor comes into play. It positions you several steps ahead of your audience and establishes you as someone worth following, not just another voice in the crowd.

Think of the X-Factor as your unique value proposition, but with a crucial twist: ***it's not just about what makes you different, but what makes you a natural leader for your specific audience.*** When you properly establish your X-Factor, readers don't just buy your books - they join your movement.

Consider Brandon Sanderson. He's not just selling fantasy novels, but an entire universe of intricate magic all while hosting a community filled with hundreds of thousands of loyal readers. His X-Factor isn't just his writing ability, but lies in his ability to make readers feel like they're part of the creative journey.

The X-Factor works by providing two critical elements: heroes to look up to and "aha moments" that transform readers' lives. These aha moments are particularly powerful because they create lasting connections.

When a reader experiences an insight or breakthrough because of your work, they're much more likely to become a loyal follower.

Your X-Factor isn't just about your credentials or achievements. It's about how you use your experience and expertise to inspire action in others. *If you've overcome significant obstacles to write your books, that journey becomes part of your X-Factor.* If you have unique professional experience that informs your writing, that's part of your X-Factor too.

The most effective way to establish your X-Factor is through what I call "leadership positioning." *This means consistently demonstrating not just what you know, but how that knowledge or experience benefits your readers.* It's about creating a clear path between your expertise and your readers' desired outcomes.

One of the hardest truths for authors to process is that none of this, not one word that you've ever written, no matter how personal, is about you. It's all about your reader using your work as a conduit to explore their own transformation.

Your X-Factor should make it clear why you're the right person to guide readers through this transformation. This might mean sharing behind-the-scenes glimpses of your creative process, explaining how your life experiences inform your writing, or demonstrating your deep understanding of the genres or topics you write about.

Importantly, your X-Factor should inspire readers to listen and take action. If you're writing historical fiction, your X-Factor might be your unique approach to research that brings forgotten stories to life. If you're writing self-help, it might be your proven method for achieving specific results.

Whatever it is, it should give readers a compelling reason to choose your work over others in your field.

The beauty of developing a strong X-Factor is that it makes marketing feel more natural. Instead of awkwardly promoting your books, you're sharing valuable insights and experiences that naturally lead readers to want more of what you offer. It transforms marketing from pushing sales to pulling readers into your world.

CONNECTION DEEPENERS

Think of Connection Deepeners as bridges between you and your readers, just not the mass-produced steel and concrete kind. These are more like handcrafted wooden bridges, each one unique, built with care and attention to the specific landscape they span.

The fascinating thing about Connection Deepeners is they work by creating resonance with your audience in ways that go beyond just books. When used effectively, they help readers feel truly seen and understood, often in ways they didn't even realize they needed.

Meeting readers where they are is crucial to this process. This means understanding that every reader comes to your work with their own context, their own struggles, their own hopes. Instead of expecting readers to adapt to your world, you're creating points of connection that feel natural and intuitive to them.

What makes Connection Deepeners particularly powerful is that they give readers a shared language to communicate with each other. ***When you create terms, phrases, or concepts that resonate with your audience, you're not just*** *building individual connections, you're fostering a community.* Consider how Terry Pratchett fans immediately understand references to "The Luggage" or how Stephen King readers share a special understanding of "The Dark Tower." These aren't just story elements, but community touchstones.

What's often overlooked is how Connection Deepeners work beyond the obvious fan-author relationship. *They create reader-to-reader bonds that strengthen your entire community.* This is why successful authors often find their readers forming book clubs, fan groups, or online communities without direct author involvement. The connections you create become self-sustaining.

The most powerful aspect of Connection Deepeners is their ability to make readers feel like their truest selves in your community. This isn't about creating a false sense of belonging - it's about providing safe spaces where readers can explore, express, and embrace who they really are. When readers feel this level of acceptance and understanding, they become more than just consumers of your work - they become active participants in your author journey.

Remember that scene in *Dead Poets Society* where students stand on their desks to see the world differently? *That's what Connection Deepeners do.* They offer new perspectives, new ways of seeing and understanding, that readers carry with them long after they've finished your books.

BUTTON-PUSHERS

Button-Pushers are those subtle yet powerful elements that transform interest into action. They're what makes someone stop scrolling, click through, and ultimately make a purchase. But they're not just about driving sales; they're about creating those magical moments where a reader thinks, "Yes, this is exactly what I've been looking for."

I call this process of realization the "snap, snap, snap." Picture what happens at a successful book signing. There's that moment when someone sees your book and something catches their eye. That's the first "snap," or ***the stop***. Then, they read the back cover or a random passage that speaks directly to them. That's the second "snap," or ***the click***. Finally, they walk to the register, book in hand. That's the third "snap," or ***the buy***. These three snaps aren't random. They're carefully orchestrated moments of connection.

What makes Button-Pushers so powerful is their ability to work at a subconscious level. ***When you use them effectively, readers don't feel pushed or manipulated. They feel drawn in, compelled by their own curiosity and desire.*** It's like creating a path of breadcrumbs that leads readers naturally to the next step.

Button-Pushers aren't about being clever or manipulative. They're about being so genuinely compelling that readers can't help but want to engage further. When you share a story that resonates deeply with your audience, when you tap into their genuine desires and aspirations, you're not pushing buttons, you're opening doors.

The real magic happens when Button-Pushers align with genuine value. Your goal isn't just to get someone to buy your book; it's to ensure they're genuinely excited to read it. Think about how Netflix gets you to watch "just one more episode" - not through force, but by understanding and delivering exactly what you want next.

Used effectively, Button-Pushers help potential readers self-identify. They think, "This author gets me," or "This is exactly what I need right now." When this happens, you've created something powerful, a connection that goes beyond the transaction to create genuine anticipation and excitement.

Remember, the ultimate goal isn't just to make the sale - it's to create such a compelling case for your work that readers can't wait to dive in. When you achieve this, marketing stops feeling like marketing and starts feeling like matchmaking between your books and their perfect readers.

UNDERSTANDING LIFE'S TRANSITIONS

Above psychological triggers, one other powerful thing to consider with your message is focusing on specific *transition points.*

Every significant change in life creates a moment of psychological openness, a time when people are more receptive to new ideas, solutions, and perspectives.

Think of transitions like a house during renovation. When the walls are stripped bare and the floors are being replaced, that's when you can make the biggest changes. Similarly, when people are going through major life transitions, their normal patterns and resistances are disrupted, creating unique opportunities for meaningful connection.

What makes transitions such powerful marketing moments? During times of change, people experience what psychologists call "identity plasticity" when their sense of self becomes more flexible and open to transformation. This isn't just about being more likely to buy. It's about being more receptive to deep, meaningful engagement with content that speaks to their current experience.

Consider the common transitions we all face: graduating from school, starting a new job, entering or leaving relationships, becoming parents, changing careers, moving cities, facing health challenges, or retiring. Each of these moments creates a psychological state where people actively seek guidance, understanding, and support. They're not just looking for solutions; they're looking for meaning and connection during times of uncertainty.

The key to leveraging transition points effectively lies in understanding their emotional architecture. Every transition contains three essential elements:

First, there's ***the letting go phase,*** where people release old patterns, identities, or situations. This often involves grief, uncertainty, and anxiety, even when the change is positive. Your marketing can acknowledge and validate these complex emotions.

Second comes the ***neutral zone***, the uncomfortable period between the old and the new. This is where people feel most vulnerable but also most open to new perspectives. Your content can provide guidance and reassurance during this crucial phase.

Finally, there's ***the new beginning*** where people establish fresh patterns and identities. This is when they're actively seeking tools, communities, and frameworks to support their emerging reality.

What makes transitions particularly powerful for marketing is that people in transition are actively engaged in self-directed change. ***They're not passive consumers waiting to be sold to, but active seekers looking for resources that speak to their experience.*** This creates natural openings for authentic connection and meaningful engagement.

Your task as a marketer is to identify which transition points align naturally with your work. What moments of change does your content speak to? When are people most likely to need what you offer? Understanding these intersections allows you to create marketing that feels less like selling and more like extending a helping hand at exactly the right moment.

EXAMPLES THAT TIE IT ALL TOGETHER

Now that we have all the pieces, let's talk about transitions and their psychological triggers in a way that feels more concrete.

THE NEW PARENT

Think about someone who's just become a new parent. They're in a massive life transition - probably sleep-deprived, overwhelmed, and questioning everything. This is a perfect moment to connect with readers because during transitions, people actively seek solutions and support. They're hungry for guidance.

Their core wound might be feeling utterly unprepared or isolated. So if you write parenting books, you don't just market your "how-to" guide. You speak to that deep feeling of uncertainty. You might share your own stumbling first weeks of parenthood (**Connection Deepener**), demonstrate your expertise through specific, relatable situations (**X-Factor**), and show the pleasure of moving from chaos to confidence.

Or consider someone going through a divorce. They're dealing with a profound sense of failure (**Core Wound**), questioning their identity, and facing an uncertain future. If you write self-discovery novels or personal growth books, this transition moment is rich with potential connection points. Your marketing might emphasize the journey from betrayal to trust, from brokenness to wholeness.

Career changes are another powerful transition point. Someone leaving corporate life to start their own business is experiencing multiple psychological triggers simultaneously, like fear of failure, dreams of independence, and a need for validation. If you write business books or even fiction about personal reinvention, this transition provides natural connection points.

The key is recognizing that transitions create openings for deeper engagement because people in transition are actively looking for:

1. Validation of their feelings
2. Guidance through uncertainty
3. Hope for the future
4. Community of others in similar situations

CAREER BURNOUT

Let's explore another powerful transition moment: career burnout. This is fascinating because it combines both professional and deeply personal psychological triggers.

Picture someone in their mid-thirties who's achieved everything they thought they wanted. They have a good job, a decent salary, and a respectable title. But they're exhausted, unfulfilled, and quietly wondering, "Is this all there is?" This transition point is particularly rich because it involves multiple core wounds: the shame of feeling ungrateful for a "good" job, the fear of starting over, and often a deep sense of betrayal (*either by the system or their choices*).

If you write inspirational fiction or career transformation books, this transition creates natural connection points. The core wound here isn't just about career frustration - it's about identity. Who are you when the career you've built stops defining you? This is where pleasure and pain inducers become incredibly powerful.

The pain points are vivid: Sunday night anxiety, feeling trapped in golden handcuffs, watching life pass by in endless Zoom meetings. But the pleasure points are equally compelling: rediscovering passion, feeling alive again, building something meaningful. Your marketing might weave these together, showing understanding of both the current pain and the potential for transformation.

Your X-Factor might come from having made this journey yourself, or from guiding others through it. You're not just offering escape; you're providing a roadmap through the wilderness of career reinvention. This resonates particularly strongly because people in career transitions are often looking for both practical guidance and emotional support.

The Connection Deepeners here could focus on shared experiences that often go unspoken - the guilt of wanting more, the fear of disappointing family, the secret relief of finally admitting you need change. When you name these experiences, readers feel seen and understood, often for the first time.

Button-Pushers in this context might focus on the cost of staying stuck versus the potential of change. Not in a manipulative way, but by reflecting real questions your readers are already asking themselves: "What's the real price of another year in this job?" "What possibilities am I never giving myself permission to explore?"

This transition point is especially powerful because it often coincides with other life transitions - relationships, health, personal identity. It's a moment when people are particularly receptive to new ideas and perspectives, making them more likely to engage deeply with content that speaks to their experience.

During career burnout transitions, people are actively seeking:

1. Validation that their dissatisfaction is legitimate and significant, not just ingratitude or weakness
2. Evidence that change is possible - not just inspirational stories, but concrete paths forward
3. Permission to prioritize fulfillment over traditional metrics of success
4. Frameworks to help them imagine and build a different future

MOVING TO A NEW CITY

Let's explore the transition of moving to a new city - a moment that combines external change with profound internal shifts.

Picture someone who's just accepted a job in a new city. On the surface, it's about logistics, like finding an apartment, learning new routes, and setting up utilities. But underneath, this person is wrestling with deeper questions about identity, community, and belonging. They're literally and figuratively mapping out a new life.

This transition is particularly rich because it often involves mourning what's left behind while simultaneously building something new. The core wound here centers on belonging - the fear of being perpetually "new," of losing established connections, of having to rebuild from scratch in an unfamiliar environment.

If you write contemporary fiction, self-help, or even city-specific guides, this transition creates powerful marketing opportunities. You're catching readers at a moment when their normal support systems are disrupted and they're actively seeking new connections and guidance. The pleasure and pain points here are deeply intertwined - the excitement of new possibilities exists alongside the anxiety of unknown challenges.

Your X-Factor might be having made multiple successful moves yourself, understanding the emotional landscape of relocation, or having deep knowledge of building community in new places. You're not just offering practical advice; you're providing emotional scaffolding for this major life change.

During relocation transitions, people are actively seeking:

1. Reassurance that their mix of excitement and grief is normal and valid
2. Practical tools for building social connections from scratch

3. Guidance on maintaining old relationships while creating new ones
4. Ways to preserve their identity while adapting to a new environment

TRANSFORMING BOOK MARKETING

As we've explored the intricate landscape of psychological marketing, one fundamental truth emerges: successful book marketing is not about selling, but about connecting. It's about creating a bridge between your work and the readers who need it most, understanding that every book is more than just a product. It's a potential transformation waiting to happen.

The strategies we've discussed—***Core Wounds, Pleasure and Pain Inducers, X-Factor, Connection Deepeners***, and ***Button-Pushers***—are not manipulative tactics, but genuine pathways to meaningful engagement. They represent a profound shift from traditional marketing approaches that treat readers as passive consumers to a more holistic model that sees readers as active participants in a shared journey.

Remember, your book is a vehicle for connection, not just information or entertainment. Every reader comes to your work with their own story, their own struggles, and their own hopes. Your marketing should honor that complexity, creating spaces where readers feel truly seen and understood.

The most powerful marketing happens when you stop trying to sell and start trying to serve. This means:

- Deeply understanding the transitions and challenges your readers face

- Sharing your authentic journey with vulnerability and courage
- Creating content that goes beyond your books to address fundamental human experiences
- Building communities that support and uplift readers

Ultimately, successful marketing is about trust. Trust that develops not through aggressive promotion, but through consistent, genuine connection. It's about showing readers that you understand them, that you're committed to their growth and transformation, and that your work is a tool for their own personal journey.

Your words have power, not just on the page, but in the lives of those who read them. Marketing, when done with empathy and insight, becomes an extension of that power. It's an invitation, a bridge, a helping hand extended to readers who are seeking something more than just another book.

So step forward with confidence. Your marketing is not about shouting into the void, but about creating meaningful dialogue. It's about turning the solitary act of writing into a collaborative experience of human connection. In a world hungry for authenticity, your genuine approach will not just sell books. It will create a lasting impact.

UNDERSTANDING THE MODERN CUSTOMER JOURNEY

Now that we've talked about the undercurrent of your marketing, it's time to sketch out how your customer goes about finding and engaging with your work. The art of turning a stranger into a loyal customer has never been more complex or more important than in today's digital landscape. Making that transition might not be a subconscious decision on the customer's part, but that customer journey should very much be front of mind as we plot out our sales process.

A customer journey represents every interaction someone has with your brand, from their first glimpse of your content to the moment they become a devoted repeat customer and beyond.

Think of it like a first date that blossoms into a long-term relationship. ***Just as you wouldn't propose marriage at first sight, you shouldn't expect an immediate purchase from someone who's just discovered your brand.*** Instead, the journey unfolds through carefully orchestrated touchpoints, each one building upon the last to create a deeper connection.

Creators who truly grasp this concept don't just see isolated interactions. Instead, they see a continuous story unfolding. Every email opened, every social media post liked, and every website visit becomes a chapter in your customer's unique narrative with your brand.

Success lies not in perfecting any single touchpoint, but in weaving them together into a coherent, compelling experience that naturally guides customers toward a lasting relationship with your brand.

Traditional marketing wisdom breaks down the customer's path into distinct stages — awareness, consideration, and decision — but modern digital tools have transformed this simple progression into something far more dynamic. Today's marketers can accelerate and enhance each stage of this journey through strategic content, targeted messaging, and perfectly timed touchpoints.

What makes contemporary marketing particularly powerful is its ability to meet customers exactly where they are in their journey. *A well-crafted strategy can transform complete strangers into interested prospects, nurture those prospects into engaged followers, and convert those followers into passionate customers who not only buy but advocate for your brand.*

Gone are the days when marketing meant shouting your message into the void and hoping the right people would hear it. Modern digital tools allow us to create personalized experiences that respond to each customer's unique needs and interests. This precision in targeting and messaging means every interaction can be more meaningful, more relevant, and ultimately more effective at moving customers along their journey.

BUILDING YOUR IDEAL CLIENT AVATAR

Before we can start building the elements of your environment, we need to know who will "live" in that environment. These are the "ideal clients" who will find your environment a perfect fit.

Think about penguins. If you bring them to the Sahara, the penguins will have a bad time, but if you put them in the chilly Antarctic, they'll be happy little buddies. The Sahara is the perfect place for camels and scorpions, though. There are no perfect environments. It's all about matching the customers with the right environment. We do that by creating an ideal client avatar.

While "ideal client avatar" sounds like marketing gibberish, it's one of the most important principles to understand if you want to build a career in the arts—or any career, frankly.

An ideal client avatar represents the person who most resonates with your message and is thus incredibly likely to buy your product. It is the virtual representation of your perfect customer.

There are two factors that come into play that help determine your ideal client avatar. The first factor is somebody who has a very high customer lifetime value. The second factor is a person with a very low customer acquisition cost.

Customer lifetime value is the amount somebody will buy from you over the course of their life. Your ideal customer will be the type of person who spends at least a hundred dollars on your products every year. This is a concept made famous by Kevin Kelly, the founding executive editor of Wired. Kelly wrote a piece on his blog in 2008 called "1,000 True Fans," which became one of the definitive pieces on building an audience with its claim that if an artist can find one thousand people willing to spend one hundred dollars a year on their work, then they can successfully make a living on their art. Even though I have issues with this theory, I hope we can all agree that generating $100,000 in income would make a very successful year.

Conversely, *customer acquisition cost* is the amount of money it costs to find a new customer and make a sale. Between tabling at conventions, sending mailing list updates, advertising, and all of the other monetary outlays that come part and parcel with finding a client, the less we spend acquiring a client means we make more money at the end of the day.

Simply put, your ideal client avatar is the person most receptive to your message and the person with whom you most want to speak.

It has to be both.

There will be people you want to speak with who have no interest in your message, and people who want to hear your message that you don't care about at all. The ideal client avatar is the beautiful merging of these two points.

So…how do we find our ideal client avatar?

First, we must find the type of people who inspire us to create. This will take some deep reflection, but you know there is a person in your life who will love your product more than anybody else. This doesn't have to be your family. It can be a friend or even somebody you aren't that close with, though I highly recommend staying inside your close friend circle at first.

Have you thought of somebody? Good. Then, let's build an avatar.

To start forming our ideal client, we need to test whether that person will be the right fit to buy what you are trying to sell. Remember, just because you want to make products for somebody doesn't mean your products will resonate with them.

To find out if somebody is a good fit, we have to look at their social media feeds for a while to see what kinds of stuff they like. We need to make sure they are buying what you are selling. If you want to make death metal pins and they are buying fluffy bunny plushies, you are barking up the wrong tree and need to start over.

What you're trying to find are the people who resonate the most with your message and love your work enough to spend bank on it for a long time.

Once you are relatively confident they buy the same type of stuff that you want to make, it's time to interview them.

It doesn't have to be anything formal, but you want feedback about why they buy what they buy. Do they like bright colors or are they more into texture? Does size matter? What is it that resonates with them when they buy something?

After you have that interview, it's time to make some different products and show them to your ideal client. This is why using an immediate friend or family member is easiest because they will be open and receptive to looking at your product. This is also why it's best not to pick your mother or anybody who will automatically love anything that you do. You want real and honest feedback about whether you are doing something that resonates with your ideal client.

This interview isn't about selling your product, but you need to know if they would buy what you are trying to sell. If you can't tell whether or not they would buy your product, push harder. This is critical research and if you get it wrong then your business will suffer and you will have to start again. You don't want to build the wrong customer avatar.

Once you've done your research, it's time to rock and roll into mass production, right? ***Absolutely and unequivocally not.***

You don't want to go into mass production just yet. After you have a good idea that your work will resonate with the right person, you need to find other people who will also be perfect fits for your product. This is the beginning of the ideal client avatar.

Create a profile of your ideal client based on your initial research. This profile needs to be as complete as you can make it. Your ideal client avatar should feel like a real person who lives and breathes. Your profile should include their name, age, ethnicity, interests, personality traits, favorite foods, favorite TV shows, favorite movies, favorite bands, favorite websites, and anything else you can think of to make your avatar feel like a real person.

Once you have the profile created, use it to find five to ten other people who fit your ideal client avatar. Replicate the same process you used before. Interview your potential customers and show them your product just as you did with the original person.

Some of the assumptions you made about your ideal client will be correct and some will be wildly misinformed. That's okay. That's how it should be. Use the new data you collected from these interviews to recreate your ideal client avatar and focus it more clearly. Your avatar will now become completer and more fleshed out because you have five to ten times the research data.

After finding five to ten people who love your product, it's time to test your ideal client avatar on people you don't know.

To do this, you need to create a small batch of products. Then, find a craft fair, comic convention, or job fair where your ideal client avatar exists in the real world. Bring your products to this event. Find people who resemble your ideal client and see if they rabidly buy what you are selling.

If they do, use your new data to compile a more complete customer avatar. If they do not, analyze why they are not buying your product, make corrections to your avatar, and try again. The more people you speak with, the more complete and real your customer avatar will become.

The stronger your ideal client avatar, the more you will be able to focus on creating a product for the right kind of person, lowering your customer acquisition cost, and increasing your lifetime customer value. Then, you can use all that data to find more people who fit that profile, which is the key to scaling your creative business.

It's also a good idea to become a consumer of the things you want to make. I meet creators all the time who don't buy the things that they sell. There is nothing wrong with this on the surface. You are not required to be your own perfect customer.

However, you should go on the journey with the customer, so you can see the world through their eyes. I have run a lot of companies in my life, and the more I used the products I was selling, the more I could understand the pain points of the customer. I understood what the customer wanted because I was the customer.

Surveying your audience is a great way to understand their needs, but there is nothing like the firsthand account of walking around a convention and seeing what catches your eye. There's nothing like reading the most popular books in your field and saying, "I liked when they did that."

By consuming the books you are writing, you develop a better understanding of what your readers like and what they don't like by experiencing them yourself.

This kind of research is invaluable to communicating with your customers. It creates an in-depth dialogue. I believe I sell 10-20 percent of my products on passion alone, but it goes deeper than that. People respond to my passion because I'm passionate about the same things they are. They know I have gone on the customer journey with them, seen what was broken, and did my best to fix it.

That last bit is important because no *customer journey* is perfect. There are wonderful things about every market, but there are also things so glaringly broken it's frustrating for people. If you understand the joy and the pain of your customer, you can make a product perfect for them, and articulate why it is perfect. That last bit is the most important part of any sale.

ANATOMY OF A CUSTOMER JOURNEY

To truly understand how customer journeys work in practice, let's follow a potential customer we'll call Bob.

Bob is digitally savvy, but also selective about where he spends both his time and money. He's experienced enough with online marketing to be skeptical of obvious sales pitches, yet he's open to authentic connections with brands that align with his interests.

One evening, while unwinding after work, Bob comes across a piece of content that catches his eye. It's a thoughtfully designed giveaway for collectors of vintage sci-fi memorabilia, one of his passionate interests that he rarely indulges. The timing is perfect; he's just finished reorganizing his collection and has been thinking about expanding it. ***This isn't just any promotional content, though.*** It's been carefully crafted to appeal to true enthusiasts, with prizes that demonstrate a real understanding of the community.

The initial touchpoint is just the beginning of Bob's journey. After clicking through, he arrives at a landing page that speaks his language, featuring references that only true fans would appreciate. The page isn't just pimping an offer to buy. It's filled with interesting content about collecting, preservation tips, and stories from other collectors. So, he signs up to the company's promotional material, what we call an "opt-in."

When he finally signs up to learn more, the experience is seamless. Instead of an abrupt "thanks for entering" message, he receives a personalized email that includes a curated guide to caring for vintage collectibles, something of genuine value whether he buys from the company or not. The brand has ***anticipated his needs and interests,*** providing relevant content before he even asks for it.

How can they do that? Because they've spent a lot of time talking to people just like Bob and know what they need, and the shared language they use to communicate with each other.

Over the next few weeks, Bob's journey continues to unfold naturally. He receives carefully timed follow-up emails, each containing valuable content rather than just promotional messages. There's an introduction to an online community of fellow collectors, exclusive interviews with notable figures in the vintage sci-fi world, and behind-the-scenes looks at rare collections. Bob finds himself increasingly engaged with the brand's content.

What makes this journey particularly effective is its organic progression. ***The brand doesn't push for a sale immediately.*** Instead, they demonstrate their expertise and value through consistently helpful content and genuine community engagement. When they do eventually present Bob with an offer—an exclusive pre-sale for a limited-edition piece—it feels less like a sales pitch and more like a natural extension of the relationship they've built.

This journey showcases several crucial elements of effective customer journey design:

1. The ***initial hook*** is precisely targeted to Bob's interests and presented at a moment when he's most receptive.
2. Each ***touchpoint*** builds upon the previous one, creating a coherent narrative rather than disconnected interactions.
3. ***Value*** is provided consistently, not just when trying to make a sale.
4. The relationship is ***nurtured*** through relevant content and community engagement.

5. The eventual ***sales offer*** is presented in context, as part of an ongoing relationship rather than a cold pitch.

By the time Bob makes his first purchase, he's not just buying a product. He's deepening his engagement with a brand that has already provided significant value. This is the essence of a well-designed customer journey: it transforms what could have been a simple transaction into a meaningful relationship that benefits both the customer and the brand.

DIFFERENT TYPES OF CUSTOMER JOURNEYS

While Bob's journey into the world of vintage collectibles illustrates one path, customer journeys are as diverse as businesses themselves. Each industry, product type, and business model demand their own unique approach to guiding customers from discovery to purchase and beyond.

While we've explored the basic framework of customer journeys, let's focus on what this means specifically for authors. The path a reader takes from discovering your book to becoming a devoted fan has its own unique characteristics and opportunities.

Consider the journey of someone discovering a new author. It might begin with a recommendation from a friend or a striking book cover that catches their eye while browsing online. They read the sample chapters, intrigued by the writing style.

Rather than immediately purchasing the book, they might follow the author on social media, discovering their background and the stories behind their stories. They sign up for the author's newsletter, receive updates about the writing process, and feel increasingly connected to the author's world. When they finally purchase and read the book, it's not just a transaction. It's the latest chapter in an ongoing relationship. This connection often leads them to eagerly await the next release, participate in book discussions, and recommend the author to other readers.

Let's now look at the journey of discovering a new favorite author. It often begins in unexpected places like a friend's enthusiastic recommendation, an intriguing review on Goodreads, or a captivating social media post about your book's theme. The potential reader might then peek at your author website, where they find not just book information, but glimpses into your writing process through blog posts or behind-the-scenes content.

The beauty of an author's customer journey lies in its emotional depth. Reading a book is an intimate experience, quite different from purchasing a typical product. Your readers aren't just buying pages bound together. They're investing hours of their time in the world you've created. This journey often starts with small commitments: following you on social media, signing up for your newsletter, or downloading a free short story. Each of these touchpoints helps build trust and familiarity with your voice as a writer.

What makes author journeys particularly special is their cyclical nature. Unlike many products where the customer journey ends with a purchase, book readers often become more invested after finishing your book. They join your reader groups, participate in book discussions, eagerly await your next release, and become advocates who recommend your work to others. Many readers actually strengthen their connection to an author between books, through interactions with your content, your community, and other readers who share their enthusiasm.

Take the example of a thriller author who understands this journey. They might start by sharing intriguing true crime stories that inspired their writing on social media, drawing in readers who share this interest.

Their newsletter might offer exclusive short stories featuring side characters from their books, keeping readers engaged between releases. They could host virtual book clubs where readers discuss not just the plot, but the deeper themes and research behind the story. Each of these touchpoints deepens the reader's connection to both the author's work and their creative world.

This deeper understanding of the reader journey helps authors move beyond simply promoting their latest release. ***Instead, they can create an ongoing relationship with readers that enriches both sides of the equation***. The goal isn't just to sell one book – it's to create a lasting connection that turns first-time readers into lifelong fans.

THE HIDDEN DEPTH OF CUSTOMER JOURNEYS

Today's customers rarely follow a straight path to purchase. They might discover your brand through a social media post, then encounter your newsletter content, while simultaneously seeing your products reviewed by their favorite influencer.

Each of these touchpoints creates a unique impression, contributing to their overall perception of your brand. It's less like a funnel and more like a constellation of connected experiences.

What makes this even more complex is the way customers move between stages. Someone might be deeply familiar with your brand but return to the research phase when considering a new product line. A loyal customer might suddenly need reassurance about their choice when a competitor launches a new offering. *These movements aren't failures of the journey, but natural patterns of human decision-making that smart brands learn to anticipate and support.*

Consider how a customer might interact with a premium skincare brand. They might first encounter the brand through a friend's recommendation, then read reviews while simultaneously following the brand's educational content about skin health. They might add products to their cart, abandon them, return to read more about ingredients, watch user testimonials, and finally make a purchase, only to start a similar journey when considering their next product. *Each of these micro-journeys contains valuable information about customer needs, hesitations, and motivations.*

The depth of customer journeys extends beyond just purchasing decisions. Every interaction leaves an emotional impression that influences future engagement. A particularly helpful customer service interaction might turn a one-time buyer into a brand advocate. A thoughtful follow-up email might transform a casual browser into a loyal customer. These emotional touchpoints often prove more valuable than traditional marketing metrics would suggest.

Digital technology has made these complex journeys both more possible and more visible. ***Customers expect brands to remember their preferences, anticipate their needs, and provide relevant information at exactly the right moment. Yet they also want these personalized experiences to feel natural and unobtrusive.*** This delicate balance requires understanding not just where customers are in their journey, but also why they're there and what might help them move forward.

The true complexity of customer journeys often reveals itself in the unusual patterns that emerge from data. One customer might engage with your high-end products for months before making their first purchase. Another might bounce between your educational content and competitor comparisons for weeks, only to become one of your most valuable customers. These patterns remind us that customer journeys are fundamentally human stories, full of the same contradictions and complexities that characterize all human decision-making.

LEARNING FROM SUCCESS STORIES

Success leaves clues, and in the publishing world, examining how successful authors build their readership offers invaluable insights into effective reader journeys. By studying these success stories, we can uncover patterns that work specifically in the book market, regardless of genre or style.

Take the approach of V.E. Schwab, who has masterfully built her readership through genuine connection. ***Beyond*** *her compelling stories, she shares her writing struggles and triumphs openly on social media, creating a sense of shared journey with her readers.* Her transparency about the creative process, combined with her engagement with fan art and reader discussions, shows how authenticity can transform readers into a passionate community.

Or consider how Leigh Bardugo has expanded her reader relationships beyond individual books. She doesn't just publish stories. She creates an immersive experience around the Grishaverse. Through thoughtful, world-building content, engaging with fan theories, and creating supplementary materials that enrich her world, she transforms readers from casual observers into invested participants in an ever-expanding universe.

Romance authors often excel at reader journey design. Authors like Talia Hibbert have built devoted followings by creating vibrant reader communities. She understands that her books aren't just standalone products but gateways to a shared experience. Through engaging social media presence, thoughtful discussion of romance tropes, and open conversations about representation in literature, she's created a space where readers feel both seen and valued.

The most successful authors understand that value must be delivered beyond the books themselves. Whether it's through thoughtful book club questions, engaging social media presence, or newsletter content that entertains as well as informs, these authors excel at creating what feels like a natural progression of engagement with their readers.

Consider how thriller author Lucy Foley builds her reader relationships. She doesn't just promote her next release. She creates carefully structured pathways that guide readers deeper into her world of mysteries. Through sharing her research process, discussing the real-world locations that inspire her settings, and engaging with readers' theories, she keeps her community engaged between books and creates multiple entry points for new readers.

Perhaps the most valuable lesson from successful authors is their ability to turn transactional relationships into emotional connections. They understand that, while an intriguing plot might initially attract readers, it's the emotional resonance of the entire experience that creates lasting loyalty.

Whether it's through personal notes to readers, sharing the challenges of the writing process, or creating special moments for their community, these connections transform ordinary reader relationships into meaningful, long-term engagement.

PLOTTING YOUR READER JOURNEY

The concept of customer journeys might sound great in theory, but how do you actually create one for your readers? Let's break down the practical steps of mapping out your reader's path from discovery to superfan.

Start with the end in mind. What do you want your ideal reader relationship to look like? Perhaps it's a devoted fan who pre-orders every book, engages in your reader community, and recommends your work to others. Or maybe it's someone who subscribes to your premium content tier and attends your virtual events. This vision becomes your journey's destination.

Now, work backwards. If we imagine your reader's experience as a series of stepping stones, each one should be a small, achievable commitment that naturally leads to the next. For example:

First Encounter → Content Sampling → First Purchase → Community Engagement → Loyal Reader → Active Advocate

For each of these stages, you'll need *three key elements*: a way for readers to find that stepping stone, clear value that makes them want to step on it, and an obvious path to the next stone. Let's break this down practically:

The *First Encounter* might happen through social media posts about your book's theme, blog posts that showcase your writing style, or newsletter swaps with similar authors. The key is making this first touch point intriguing enough for readers to want more.

Content Sampling could be the first few chapters available on your website, a free prequel novella, or exclusive short stories. This gives readers a risk-free way to experience your writing and connect with your style.

The path to *First Purchase* needs to be crystal clear. Your sample content should lead naturally to information about your full books, with easy links to purchase. Consider offering a special incentive for newsletter subscribers, like bonus epilogues or character interviews.

Community Engagement might start small – encouraging readers to follow your social media or join your reader group. Make sure you're offering value here too, whether it's behind-the-scenes content, early cover reveals, or simple engagement with fellow fans.

The transition to **Loyal Reader** often happens through consistent delivery of both books and supplementary content. This might include exclusive newsletter content, special editions for subscribers, or early access to new releases.

Finally, **Active Advocates** emerge when you make it easy and rewarding to spread the word about your books. This could be through shareable content, referral rewards, or simply by creating such a compelling experience that readers naturally want to tell others.

Remember to install feedback mechanisms at each stage. Analytics tools, reader surveys, and direct conversations with your audience can help you understand where readers might be getting stuck or losing interest in their journey.

Most importantly, **be patient.** Building these pathways takes time, and it's okay to start small. Focus on creating one clear path first, then expand and refine based on what you learn from your readers' behavior and feedback.

THE FUTURE OF CUSTOMER JOURNEYS

As we look toward the horizon of customer experience, the evolution of customer journeys is accelerating at an unprecedented pace. Artificial intelligence and machine learning are transforming what's possible in journey personalization, while changing consumer expectations are reshaping how brands need to interact with their audiences.

The future of customer journeys is being dramatically reshaped by technologies that can predict and respond to customer needs in real time. Imagine a journey that automatically adapts based on subtle signals in customer behavior and offers not just based on past actions, but on predicted future needs. This isn't science fiction; it's already happening in pioneering companies that use AI to craft uniquely personalized experiences for each customer.

Yet amidst this technological revolution, we're witnessing a counterintuitive trend: the rising importance of human connection.

As **automation** becomes more prevalent, customers increasingly value authentic, human-centered interactions. The most successful brands of tomorrow will be those that master this balance—using technology to enable more meaningful human connections rather than replace them.

Privacy considerations are also reshaping how we think about customer journeys. With growing awareness and regulation around data usage, brands must become more transparent and intentional about how they collect and use customer information. The future belongs to companies that can create compelling, personalized experiences while respecting and protecting customer privacy.

Future customer journeys won't be defined by platform or device but will flow naturally across touchpoints, following customers through their daily lives. Voice interfaces, augmented reality, and ambient computing will create new types of interactions that feel less like traditional marketing and more like helpful companions on the customer's path.

Perhaps most significantly, we're seeing a shift toward what might be called "journey co-creation," where customers have more control over how they interact with brands.

Rather than following predetermined paths, customers will increasingly expect to shape their own journeys, choosing how and when they engage with brands. This requires a fundamental rethinking of how we design customer experiences, moving from linear journeys to more flexible, customer-directed experiences.

The rise of community-driven commerce is another force shaping future customer journeys. Brands are becoming platforms for connection, where the value comes not just from the product or service but from the community of users around it. This transforms the traditional customer journey into something more collaborative and social, where peer interactions become as important as brand communications.

As we look ahead, one thing becomes clear: the future of customer journeys will be defined not by the technologies we use, but by how well we use them to serve genuine human needs and desires. Success will come to brands that can harness these new capabilities while staying true to the timeless principles of human connection, trust, and value creation.

In today's complex digital landscape, the brands that thrive aren't necessarily those with the biggest budgets or the most advanced technology. Instead, *they're the ones that understand how to weave together meaningful experiences that resonate with their customers' lives.* They recognize that every email, every social media interaction, and every customer service call is an opportunity to strengthen the relationship between brand and customer.

In the end, the most successful customer journeys aren't those that simply lead to a purchase. They're the ones that leave customers feeling understood, valued, and eager to continue their relationship with your brand. As we move forward into an increasingly complex and connected world, this human-centered approach to customer journeys will become not just an advantage, but a necessity.

FUNNELS VS. FLYWHEELS

In the opening chapter, we talked about funnels and flywheels a bit, but now we're going to delve deep into how to make them work for your business. For years, authors have relied on the funnel model to sell books. The idea is simple:

- You attract potential readers at the top
- Guide them through a structured path, and eventually
- Convert them into buyers at the bottom

It's a straight-line approach. You bring people in, move them through, and hope they come out the other side with their credit cards open. It's worked for decades because it simplifies marketing. You know where someone is on their buying journey, and you can tailor your messaging accordingly.

The problem with funnels is that they assume once a reader reaches the bottom, the job is done. That's rarely the case. A one-time buyer isn't necessarily a long-term fan, and if your entire business depends on constantly refilling the funnel with new people, you're running on a treadmill that never stops. Funnels work, but they burn people out. Running ads, optimizing conversions, tweaking landing pages, it's all so exhausting. And the moment you stop? The whole system grinds to a halt.

The traditional marketing funnel is designed to be a linear path. Someone discovers your book, they express interest, consider it, and then buy, but books aren't a one-and-done product. Whether it's a novel, a series, or an entire catalog of work, these aren't disposable items like a one-time purchase of a blender. If someone loves your book, they don't just want one. They want more. The funnel ignores that and sees each customer as a single transaction, not a long-term reader who could become an advocate for your work.

When you launch a new book, you probably use a mix of paid advertising, social media buzz, email marketing, and retailer algorithms to push traffic toward your Amazon page or direct sales site. That's a funnel in action. It works well for launches because it provides a clear sequence: discovery, engagement, decision, purchase. You can measure ad clicks, track open rates on emails, and see exactly how many people are making it through the process. That's why so many authors stick with funnels. It gives the illusion of control. You put X dollars into ads, and Y number of readers come out the other side.

But what happens after that launch window? If all your effort goes into attracting new buyers and there's no system in place to keep them engaged, then every time you publish a book, you're starting from zero. That's exhausting. And it's one of the biggest reasons authors burn out.

The reality is that relying on a funnel alone makes it impossible to build a sustainable career. There are always diminishing returns. Your best-performing ads will eventually become more expensive. Your email list will stagnate if you're only sending promotions. Retailer algorithms constantly change, and you have zero control over them. If the only thing keeping your sales afloat is the constant churn of new readers, then you're at the mercy of external forces you can't control.

Funnels are still useful. They're great for getting readers in the door. But you need something else to keep them there.

You need a way to ensure that once someone reads one book, they want to read them all. That's where the flywheel comes in.

A funnel is a way to capture attention, but it doesn't retain it. A flywheel is built on momentum, where every new reader you bring in strengthens your ecosystem instead of just exiting at the bottom of a sales pipeline. The best author businesses aren't built on pure acquisition. They're built on retention, engagement, and advocacy. Funnels alone won't get you there, but pairing them with a flywheel will.

Once a reader is in your system, the goal should be to keep them engaged, not just sell them a single book. That means nurturing them with content they care about, giving them reasons to stay invested in your brand, and making them feel like they're part of something bigger than just a single transaction. If you've ever seen an author with a wildly devoted fanbase, this is what they're doing, whether they know it or not. They aren't just selling books. They're building a system that makes readers want to stick around for the long haul.

Funnels work in the short term. But flywheels make your business sustainable. And if you can learn to use both together, you won't just sell books, you'll build a long-term author career that doesn't rely on constant hustle.

FLYWHEELS: HOW MOMENTUM MAKES SELLING EASIER

If funnels are about getting readers in the door, flywheels are about keeping them inside, engaged, and eager for more. The traditional marketing funnel focuses on moving potential customers from awareness to purchase, but what happens after that? That's where a flywheel comes in. Instead of treating readers as one-time buyers, a flywheel turns them into repeat customers, superfans, and advocates who help fuel your career long after the initial sale.

A flywheel is a self-sustaining system where each reader you attract contributes to long-term growth. Think of it like a spinning wheel. When you first push it, it takes effort to get going, but once it builds momentum, it continues turning with much less force. Every time a reader buys another book, backs a Kickstarter, or recommends your work to a friend, they keep the flywheel spinning, making it easier to generate sales in the future.

The key difference between a funnel and a flywheel is retention. Funnels assume customers will leave after making a purchase, requiring constant replenishment. Flywheels, on the other hand, keep readers engaged so they don't just buy once. Instead, they stick around, read more books, and become part of your ecosystem. This approach makes your business far more sustainable in the long run.

HOW A FLYWHEEL WORKS FOR AUTHORS

There are three core components to an author's flywheel: **Attract, Engage, and Delight.** These elements work together to create a continuous loop that feeds itself over time.

- **Attract** – This is the part where new readers discover you. It could be through ads, a viral social media post, a BookBub promotion, or word of mouth. Attracting new readers isn't just about marketing. It's about making your books so compelling that readers naturally spread the word.

- **Engage** – Once a reader finds you, the next step is keeping them engaged. That might mean offering a free short story, inviting them to your newsletter, or creating bonus content that keeps them invested in your world. The goal is to make sure they don't just read one book and disappear.

- **Delight** – This is where true fan-building happens. If you can exceed reader expectations whether through personal engagement, great storytelling, or special offers, they're more likely to become lifelong fans. Delighted readers don't just buy more books; they tell others about your work, keeping the flywheel spinning.

THE POWER OF RETENTION: WHY FLYWHEELS BEAT FUNNELS IN THE LONG RUN

Retention is where most authors struggle. Many writers focus so much on acquiring new readers that they forget about the ones they already have. But a loyal reader who sticks with you over multiple books is far more valuable than constantly chasing new customers. With a strong flywheel, every new reader becomes a long-term asset rather than a one-off sale.

A well-run flywheel does a few things exceptionally well:

- **It increases lifetime value.** Instead of earning a few dollars from one sale, you build relationships that result in readers buying your entire catalog over time.

- **It reduces marketing costs.** Satisfied readers refer others, reducing the need for expensive ads and promotions.
- **It compounds over time.** A strong fanbase becomes an ongoing source of revenue, making each new book launch easier than the last.

BUILDING AN EFFECTIVE FLYWHEEL AS AN AUTHOR

To get a flywheel running, you need to think beyond single book sales and focus on **building a system that keeps readers engaged.** Here's how to put the key components into practice:

1. **Create an Easy Entry Point:** Not everyone will start with your latest book, so you need an entry point that hooks readers and brings them into your ecosystem. This could be a **permafree** first-in-series, a discounted box set, or an exclusive story available only on your website. The goal is to **reduce friction** and make it as easy as possible for someone to say yes to your work.
2. **Build a Strong Engagement System:** Once a reader buys a book, what happens next? Many authors simply hope they'll return for the next one, but a flywheel requires **active engagement.** This means:
   - Encouraging sign-ups for your **newsletter** with exclusive content.
   - Sending automated emails that guide readers through your catalog.
   - Engaging on social media in a way that invites participation and discussion.
3. **Overdeliver on Experience:** Readers expect a certain level of quality from books they buy. But to turn casual readers into superfans, you have to **surprise and delight them.** That could mean:

- Offering signed editions or special bundles for direct sales.
- Running community-driven events (like live Q&As, behind-the-scenes content).
- Making sure your books consistently exceed expectations in storytelling and presentation.

Some of the best author flywheels involve **membership models, ongoing engagement, and strong branding.** Look at how Brandon Sanderson engages his fanbase with Kickstarters, or how indie authors like R.J. Blain use communities to keep readers excited about their books.

If readers know there's always something new and exciting happening in your ecosystem, they'll want to stay involved.

HOW A FLYWHEEL SAVES YOU FROM BURNOUT

Authors who rely only on funnels feel like they're constantly starting from scratch. They have to market every new book like it's their first because they don't have a system keeping past readers engaged. This is exhausting and unsustainable.

A flywheel removes this problem by making each launch easier than the last. When you have a dedicated reader base, they're already **waiting** for your next book. You don't need to spend as much on ads, run as many promotions, or stress about whether people will buy. The audience is already there, and they're ready to support you.

If you're used to thinking in terms of funnels, shifting to a flywheel mindset might take time. The key is **building systems that nurture long-term relationships.** Instead of focusing only on immediate sales, start asking:

- How can I keep readers engaged between book launches?
- What experience am I offering beyond just a book purchase?
- How am I rewarding and acknowledging my most loyal fans?

By answering these questions, you'll start to see where your flywheel needs improvement. Maybe your newsletter needs better onboarding. Maybe your backlist isn't well-promoted. Maybe you're not interacting with your audience in a way that makes them feel valued. The stronger your flywheel, the less effort you'll need to sustain sales over time.

Flywheels aren't a replacement for funnels. They're an extension of them. Funnels bring people in, but a flywheel ensures they stay. By focusing on retention, engagement, and advocacy, you can build a system that makes your business stronger with every book you release.

For authors, this means less stress, more sustainable sales, and a fanbase that actually grows over time instead of resetting with each new launch. If you want to sell books without constantly feeling like you have to start over, a flywheel is the missing piece. And in the next section, we'll explore exactly how to combine funnels and flywheels to get the best of both worlds.

Funnels and flywheels aren't competing strategies. They're complementary. The best author businesses use both. Funnels to acquire new readers and flywheels to keep them engaged. A funnel without a flywheel is a treadmill. A flywheel without a funnel is a stagnant pond. The real magic happens when you integrate the two into a cohesive system.

A funnel helps you get attention and turn strangers into buyers. A flywheel keeps those buyers engaged, so they buy more and bring in new readers for you. This is the difference between constantly scrambling for new sales and having a system that works for you even when you're not actively launching a book.

Authors who only focus on funnels end up exhausted. Every book release feels like starting from scratch. They need new ads, new promotions, and new strategies because their past readers aren't sticking around.

Authors who only focus on flywheels might struggle to grow their audience. If you're not actively attracting new readers, your system will eventually slow down. Even the best flywheels need new energy to keep them spinning.

But together? That's where the magic happens.

A well-structured funnel feeds a flywheel. A strong flywheel makes future funnels easier. Readers enter through your funnel, become part of your community, and then fuel your flywheel by engaging with your books, recommending you to others, and keeping your business moving.

HOW TO INTEGRATE FUNNELS AND FLYWHEELS IN YOUR AUTHOR BUSINESS

You don't have to pick between a funnel and a flywheel. They're not competing strategies, but are meant to work together, each serving a different but essential role in growing your audience.

A funnel brings in new readers, moving them from strangers to buyers, while a flywheel keeps them engaged so they stick around for the long haul. When you have both working in sync, every reader who discovers you has the potential to become a long-term fan, not just a one-time customer.

It all starts with the **funnel**, which is designed to take someone from, *"Who's this?"* to *"I need to buy this book right now."* Maybe they see an ad for a permafree book, a discounted box set, or a special promotion on a retailer site. That's the entry point. They click, download, and now they're inside your world, but at this stage, they're just curious. They don't know you yet, and they have no emotional investment in your books. That's why the next step is crucial.

Instead of hoping they'll come back for more, you guide them to the answer you (and they) want, which is to buy your books. A well-structured funnel doesn't end with a free book, it builds a relationship. Once they've grabbed their first book, they're invited to sign up for your newsletter, where they start receiving emails that do more than just push sales. These emails introduce them to your writing style, share your inspirations, and let them know what to expect if they stick with you. It's not about bombarding them with offers, but about **building trust** and making them feel like they've found an author worth following.

As they move through this experience, something shifts. They stop being just a casual downloader and start becoming an invested reader. Maybe they finish that first book and get an email pointing them toward the next one. Maybe they get a personal note from you, thanking them for signing up. Maybe they receive behind-the-scenes content or an exclusive bonus story that makes them feel like they're part of something special.

Then comes the moment when they make their first real purchase. Not just a free download, but a book they actively choose to buy. And when that happens, they're no longer just a name on a list. They've entered your flywheel, where they'll keep coming back, discovering more of your books, and becoming part of your long-term readership.

That's the beauty of a system where funnels and flywheels work together. Instead of constantly chasing new readers who disappear after one book, you're capturing their attention and keeping them engaged, making every sale the beginning of something bigger.

Once a reader buys their first book, what happens next? This is the moment where most authors lose potential superfans; not because the book wasn't good, but because there's no structured way to keep that reader engaged. The assumption is that if someone enjoys a book, they'll naturally seek out the next one. But in reality? Most readers don't. Life gets in the way, distractions pop up, and unless you actively guide them back to your world, they may never return.

That's why a flywheel isn't something that spins on its own. It needs momentum. A reader finishing one book doesn't automatically mean they'll buy the next, but a small **nudge in the right direction** can make all the difference. Maybe it's a simple email that lands in their inbox right after they finish reading, pointing them toward the next book in the series. Maybe it's an **exclusive bonus scene** or behind-the-scenes content that makes them feel like they're getting something special.

For some, it's about **community**, like being invited into a private Facebook group, a Discord server, or a reader club where they can connect with you and other fans. That sense of belonging turns casual readers into die-hard supporters. Others might be drawn in by **special deals** like a limited-time bundle, an exclusive hardcover edition, or a personalized bookplate that makes their purchase feel unique.

And then there's the power of **asking for feedback**. A simple, well-timed request for a review or even a personal note thanking them for reading can deepen their investment in your work. Readers who feel seen, valued, and appreciated don't just come back for more, but they start **spreading the word**. They become part of your ecosystem, recommending your books to friends, engaging with your content, and fueling the momentum of your flywheel.

Each one of these small touchpoints strengthens their connection to you as an author, making it far more likely that they'll not only buy again but **stick around for the long haul**. That's how a flywheel works, not through random chance, but through **intentional engagement** that keeps readers moving forward.

Most authors believe random chance will save them, and while I'm also about falling into the chaos of the universe, doing so with intention will always beat allowing yourself to be caught up in the chaos of the universe, at least for your bank account.

KEEP THE FLYWHEEL SPINNING WITH ONGOING ENGAGEMENT

Once readers are inside your flywheel, your job is to **keep them engaged.** If they read one book but never return, the flywheel dies. If they stay involved, it speeds up.

Keeping your flywheel spinning isn't about constantly selling. It's about **staying connected** with your readers in a way that makes them want to stick around. It starts with communication. If the only time you reach out is when you have something to sell, readers will start tuning you out. But if you're consistently delivering value, whether that's through behind-the-scenes updates, insights into your creative process, or simply sharing things you know they'll love, then your emails become something they look forward to, not just another sales pitch.

Beyond that, giving readers **special access** can deepen their connection to your work. When someone feels like they're getting something exclusive—early access to a book, a signed edition, or a sneak peek at what's coming next— they're far more likely to stay engaged. These little perks don't just make them feel valued; they make them **part of the journey**.

The strongest flywheels don't just rely on a passive audience, they create **community**. Whether that's through a private Facebook group, a Discord server, or a Patreon membership, giving readers a space to interact with you (and with each other) makes your world feel bigger than just the books. When readers have a place to connect, discuss, and share their excitement, they're no longer just fans—they're part of something bigger.

It's important to note here that you can have a very quiet community that loves you dearly. I barely get any interaction on my posts or articles, yet almost 200 people flew to NOLA in March 2025 because they loved our work, and told me how much my work meant to them, even though they almost never comment. Most readers engage through the work, not around it. Think about your favorite movies, albums, or even books. How many of those creators do you follow and engage with on a regular basis? Probably not many.

And finally, not every reader will enter your world the same way. Some will find you through your books, but others might discover you through a short story, a Kickstarter campaign, or a limited-time offer. By giving readers multiple ways to step into your ecosystem, you're increasing the chances that once they do, they'll **stick around for the long haul**.

Flywheels aren't about selling **one** book. They're about making sure that once a reader enters your ecosystem, they never want to leave.

THE REAL REASON SOME AUTHORS BURN OUT (AND HOW THIS FIXES IT)

If you feel like every book launch is an uphill battle, it's probably because **you're only running funnels and not a flywheel.** Authors who depend entirely on launch spikes and retailer promotions are caught in a cycle of **constant hustle.** They have to keep pushing because nothing is keeping readers engaged once they buy.

A properly built flywheel changes everything about how you sell books. Instead of every new launch feeling like a desperate scramble for attention, you already have a group of readers waiting for your next release. These aren't strangers who stumbled across an ad. They're people who have already bought from you, already trust you, and are already eager for more.

Each new reader that comes into your world doesn't just disappear after one purchase. They stick around, moving deeper into your ecosystem, engaging with your content, and becoming long-term fans. Over time, this means that marketing gets easier, not harder. You're not constantly starting from scratch, trying to convince cold audiences to take a chance on you. Instead, you're building momentum where every book you sell makes the next one easier to sell.

And the best part? You don't have to rely on endless promotions just to stay relevant. Instead of fighting against retailer algorithms or constantly throwing money at ads, your audience itself becomes a source of growth. Readers spread the word, tell their friends, and support you in ways that are more powerful than any marketing strategy. Your business continues to grow, even when you're not actively launching a new book, because the energy of your existing readers keeps the flywheel turning.

By shifting from one-time transactions to **ongoing relationships**, you're no longer just selling books. You're creating a world readers want to return to, again and again. By integrating a flywheel, you shift from **one-time transactions** to **ongoing relationships.** Readers don't just buy your book. They become part of your world.

HOW TO BALANCE THE TWO FOR MAXIMUM RESULTS

Getting the balance right is key. Here's how to structure your strategy:

1. **Prioritize funnels for growth periods.** When launching a new book or running a big promotion, your focus should be on attracting **new** readers. This is when ads, newsletter swaps, and outreach are most useful.
2. **Strengthen your flywheel between launches.** Once new readers enter your system, shift gears. Instead of constantly chasing new leads, focus on keeping the ones you already have engaged.
3. **Measure success beyond just sales.** Instead of only tracking book sales, monitor engagement metrics like email open rates, community interactions, and repeat purchases.
4. **Make it easy for readers to move through your ecosystem.** If they finish a book, there should be **zero friction** between that and the next book. Backmatter links, automated emails, and personal engagement all help with this.

When you combine a well-structured funnel with a strong flywheel, your author business stops feeling like a grind. Instead of constantly starting over, you're building something that compounds over time. Every book launch gets easier. Every new reader increases your momentum. Your marketing becomes less about chasing new buyers and more about keeping the ones you already have.

And the best part? You're no longer at the mercy of Amazon's algorithms, ad prices, or social media changes. Your readers aren't just buying books. They're part of a system that sustains your career.

This is the shift from selling books to building a business, and once you make it, everything gets easier. If funnels are about short-term sales, flywheels are about long-term success. Using both ensures you're not just selling books, you're creating a career that lasts.

HOW THIS MODEL SUPERCHARGES BOTH FUNNELS AND FLYWHEELS

Most authors start their careers believing the only way to sell books is through retailers like Amazon, Apple Books, Barnes & Noble, or Kobo. That's what everyone teaches. Get your books on these platforms, hope for a strong algorithm boost, run ads, and pray that sales keep coming. But after a few years in the game, many authors realize something is off. They're working harder than ever—pouring money into ads, stressing over algorithm changes, constantly launching and relaunching—but they aren't building anything that lasts.

Direct sales change that.

When you sell books directly to your audience, everything about your business shifts. Suddenly, you're not fighting for visibility on someone else's platform or hoping that Amazon decides to show your book to the right readers. Instead, you're in control. You know who your customers are, you can reach them whenever you want, and every sale means more money in your pocket.

At first, selling direct might sound like more work. Setting up a storefront, handling customer support, and driving your own traffic all feels like adding another full-time job. But when you zoom out and look at the long-term impact, the benefits become impossible to ignore. Authors who embrace direct sales stop living launch to launch. They stop depending on fleeting spikes in retailer visibility and start building something sustainable.

It's not just about revenue, though money is a major factor. When you sell direct, you're not giving 30-70% of your earnings to a middleman. That means a $10 ebook sale through your own store is worth two, sometimes three times what you'd get from Amazon. Over time, that difference is game-changing. An author making $50,000 a year on Amazon would make closer to $100,000 if they transitioned even part of their sales to a direct model. That's the kind of shift that turns a side hustle into a full-time career.

But money alone isn't the biggest reason to sell direct. The real power is in the relationship. On Amazon, you don't know who your customers are. They buy your book, and then they disappear into the void. Maybe they buy the next one, maybe they don't. You have no way to follow up, no way to keep them engaged, no way to turn a casual reader into a lifelong fan. So, you have no control.

That's where most authors lose out, because a career isn't built on one-time buyers. It's built on readers who stick around, who buy everything you write, who tell their friends about your books and back your Kickstarter projects.

Direct sales makes that possible.

When someone buys from your store, you don't just get their money. You get their email, their attention, and a direct line of communication. You can send them a thank-you message, offer them a bonus, tell them about your next book. You can guide them deeper into your world. Instead of leaving that connection up to chance, you control it. That's where the funnel and the flywheel come together, direct sales make both stronger.

When you run a Facebook ad to a retailer, what happens? If you send that traffic to Amazon, you might get some sales. But that's it. You have no idea who bought, and you can't reach them again unless you keep running ads. Every sale is a dead end. But if that same ad sends readers to your own store, you now have a direct relationship with them. You can follow up, offer them the next book in the series, and introduce them to your other work. Every sale feeds your ecosystem instead of disappearing into a retailer's algorithm.

This shift doesn't just make marketing easier, it makes everything about your business more sustainable. Instead of relying on platforms you don't control, you're building an audience that's truly yours. You're creating a system where each book launch gets easier, where every sale fuels the next, where your readers become part of something bigger than just a single transaction.

Some authors worry that selling direct means losing retailer sales, but that's not the case. In reality, the two models can work together. You don't have to pull your books from Amazon or stop using Kindle Unlimited to start selling direct. I know plenty of authors who are in KU with ebooks but wide with print books and audiobooks. It's not an either/or decision. It's "Yes, and I'll have that too, please," as Renee Rose says.

You just need to make it a priority. Give your readers a reason to buy from you. Maybe that's early access to new releases, special editions, signed copies, or behind-the-scenes content. The more value you offer, the more likely they are to choose your store over a retailer.

And once they do? They're yours forever.

For authors who make this transition, the change is profound. Instead of scrambling for visibility every time a book launches, they have an audience waiting. Instead of spending thousands on ads with no guarantee of future sales, they're investing in relationships that last. Their business stops being about survival and starts being about growth.

That's the power of direct sales. It doesn't just give you better margins, it gives you control over your future. And in a world where algorithms change overnight, that control is priceless.

HOW TO STRUCTURE YOUR AUTHOR BUSINESS FOR LONG-TERM SUCCESS

Selling books isn't just about writing them. If it were, every talented author would be rolling in money, but we know that's not the case. What separates struggling writers from those who build thriving, sustainable careers isn't just talent, it's strategy. It's understanding how to connect with readers, how to keep them engaged, and how to create a system that works even when you're not actively launching something new.

That's what this whole framework—funnels, flywheels, and book sales—is about in the end. It's not a magic bullet. It won't make you an overnight success. But what it will do is set you up for consistent, predictable, long-term growth so you're not constantly scrambling to make your next book sell. It turns your career from a series of unpredictable spikes into a steady, compounding business that grows over time.

The hardest part of being an author isn't writing. It's figuring out how to make sales sustainable. For most authors, book launches feel like a mad sprint. You spend months writing, then throw everything you have into marketing for a few weeks, praying it pays off. Sometimes it works. Sometimes it doesn't. But either way, the moment you stop pushing, sales start to drop. And if you don't have another book ready to go, you're back at square one. That cycle is exhausting. It's why so many authors burn out.

The better way is to build a system where every book you sell strengthens your business instead of just keeping it afloat. That means having a funnel that brings new readers in, a flywheel that keeps them engaged, and a direct sales strategy that ensures every book you sell is more than just a one-time transaction.

When you run a smart funnel, every new reader you attract isn't just a single sale. They're the beginning of a potential long-term relationship. You're not relying on retailers to introduce you to readers; you're bringing them directly into your world. You're capturing their email, giving them a reason to stay connected, and setting the stage for future sales.

When you have a strong flywheel, you're not just throwing books into the void, hoping people buy them. You're actively keeping readers engaged. You're giving them reasons to stay in your orbit—whether that's through an active newsletter, a reader community, bonus content, or behind-the-scenes access. Readers aren't just stumbling onto your books and leaving; they're sticking around.

When you sell direct, you're making sure that every sale is worth more. You're not just getting a royalty check. You're getting customer data, control over pricing, the ability to upsell and cross-sell, and the chance to turn one-time buyers into lifelong fans. You're reducing your dependence on platforms you don't control. You're building something that's yours.

This is how successful authors make it work. They don't just rely on Amazon's algorithm. They don't just keep throwing money at ads, hoping for the best. They create systems that make every sale easier than the last.

The authors who build six- and seven-figure careers don't do it because they write more books than everyone else. They do it because they turn every book they write into an asset that keeps working for them.

- Instead of treating every launch like a fresh start, they build an audience that grows with every release.
- Instead of betting everything on retailer promotions, they create direct connections with readers so they aren't constantly at the mercy of shifting algorithms.
- Instead of hustling for every single sale, they build a business that compounds over time, where each new reader is more than just a one-time buyer—they're part of a system that keeps their career moving forward.

This is how you stop feeling like you're always chasing the next sale. It's how you stop burning out from launch after launch. It's how you finally create a business that feels sustainable instead of like a never-ending grind.

The hardest part of this shift isn't understanding it, but committing to it. It's deciding that you're not just an author who writes books and hopes they sell. You're a business owner. You're in control of your career. And that means making intentional choices about how you sell, how you market, and how you engage with your readers.

That might mean investing time into learning how to sell direct instead of relying solely on Amazon. It might mean rethinking your marketing strategy so it's not just about finding new readers but also about keeping the ones you already have. It might mean prioritizing engagement and retention instead of constantly chasing visibility.

But the result? A business that grows without burning you out. A system that works even when you're not launching. A career that isn't dependent on ad spend or retailer favor.

Most importantly, a reader base that keeps coming back, book after book, year after year.

That's the goal. That's the shift that changes everything. And the authors who make it? They don't just sell books.

They build something that lasts.

THE GROWTH-TO-MONETIZATION PARALLEL FOR WRITERS

Before we (finally) get into the stack, I'd like to introduce you to *the growth-to-monetization parallel.*

On one end of this parallel, you have growth. In order to grow your audience, you need to invest in marketing to get in front of them and reduce friction to hook them. Basically, you have to give stuff away to lots of people for free by spending lots of money.

At the other end of this spectrum, you are trying to maximize your money in the bank to keep your business running and pay your bills, which means paywalling content, raising prices, and severely *increasing* friction.

These two actions consume most business actions, and it's nearly impossible for a small business to do both at the same time. Each of us lies somewhere on the growth to monetization parallel, but it's a bit nebulous where for most of us, most of the time.

I'll bet you have never thought about this spectrum before. Heck, I only *just* realized it existed and this is as close to a job as I have in my life.

…which isn't great, since if you don't know how to judge both your current position and where you'd like to be, you will be likely to make decisions against your best interests, and thus get frustrated and stay broke.

Once you understand this parallel and give context to it, though, hopefully you can make better decisions in your business moving forward.

GROWTH PHASE

For most writers, their initial focus is on building an audience, or even just growing as a writer who can create content consistently, sharing your work widely, and engaging with readers to build a loyal following. These types of writers are heavily indexing for growth, knowing that in order to be read they have to be found.

However, this growth-focused approach comes with financial sacrifices. In fact, you are almost always undercutting your money situation in a growth phase because you're almost always giving at least some portion of your work for free.

Maybe it's just a story or maybe it's whole books, but growth is about removing friction, and the biggest friction point to somebody reading your work is spending money on it.

Many self-published authors on platforms like Wattpad or AO3 start by sharing their work for free. These platforms allow them to reach a broad audience, but monetization opportunities may be limited initially. As their stories gain traction and readership grows, these authors often transition to monetization strategies like offering paid versions of their books, setting up Patreon accounts, or selling exclusive content.

However, this problem exists even with writers who build a big, engaged audience. Sometimes, successful people are actually struggling financially even harder than newbie authors under the weight of all their expenses. Many leverage all their time and resources to maintain audience growth, leaving little room for income-generating activities. The illusion of success, driven by high follower counts or large subscriber lists, can mask brutal (and unstable) financial instability.

Bloggers and social media influencers who amass large followings often face this challenge. While they may have millions of subscribers or followers, the income generated from ads, affiliate marketing, or donations may not be enough to sustain them. The pressure to continually produce free content to maintain and grow their audience can lead to burnout, especially when the financial returns are minimal.

Meanwhile, if they stop hustling, so does the growth of their channel, which puts them in a very dangerous doom loop, especially as they try to change their content to appeal to a broader audience.

MONETIZATION PHASE

After writers build their audience, their focus eventually shifts from growth to monetization—finding ways to generate income from the readership they've cultivated. This might involve introducing paid content, offering services like editing or coaching, launching a Patreon, or selling books directly to their audience.

Money is great. I especially like the act of exchanging it for things we need and want, but most authors have trouble simply asking people to financially support their work. Even if a writer grows comfortable with selling their work, it's a tricky balance to maintain, especially when many people are only in your audience for the free stuff.

Plus, nothing kills growth like monetization. I run a lot of launch events, and I always lose the most subscribers when I'm promoting one, which means I have to make a concerted effort to grow my audience and nurture them once the event is done.

On the other side, if you're giving away too much for free, you are undercutting your own revenue. So, you end up with a volatile and precarious balancing act that you're trying to walk at all times, but especially during a monetization event.

THE BALANCING ACT

Successfully navigating the growth-to-monetization parallel as a writer involves finding the right balance between expanding your audience and generating revenue. Here are some strategies to consider:

Time-limited sales: Introduce sales for a limited time to your audience, like through Kickstarter or an event, which allows you to focus on monetization for a little while and then return to your regular content. PBS pledge drives are famous for this strategy. The problem with this is that you will lose a lot of subscribers as people turn away from your work as you try to sell it.

Market Segmentation: Offer different levels of access or content to your audience. For example, you can provide free blog posts while reserving in-depth articles, exclusive stories, or behind-the-scenes content for paying subscribers.

Maintaining Reader Trust: It's essential to ensure that monetization efforts don't alienate your readers. Be transparent about why you're introducing paid content and ensure that it complements, rather than replaces, the free content your audience has come to love.

Set a goal: A lot of creators set a subscriber goal before they monetize, and then make a big event out of it, so it's part of a celebration. Sales events should be celebrations both of the work and of the audience that helped build it.

Sustainability and Burnout Prevention: It's crucial to strike a balance that allows you to sustain both your audience growth and your income over the long term. Avoid the temptation to continually increase free content production without adequate compensation, as this can lead to burnout.

The growth-to-monetization parallel is not just a one-time challenge but a continuous, fluid process that ebbs and flows throughout a writer's career.

Sustainability is key in this journey. Writers need to recognize that growth and monetization are not distinct phases but intertwined elements of their ongoing career. The balance between expanding an audience and monetizing that growth is something that evolves over time, requiring constant adjustment and adaptation. Monica Leonelle made a great point about this:

There's sustainability around productivity and sustainability around money. And these two things can't be uncoupled for the most part. Energetically one begets the other as it stands in the most prominent business models for authors.

A lot of authors are working on one or the other or both. But no one or at least not many are saying, "Hey, maybe these prominent business models are not the answer and were never particularly sustainable for most people."

Sure, you can have a sustainable production system but you aren't going to plug that into an unsustainable business model and get sustainable money. And many discussions about this still feel suspicious because we can all see and feel that.

Without sustainable patterns for both growth and monetization, we are all at risk of burning out all the time.

AN EXAMPLE PROVING MY POINT

We've talked a lot about how growth and monetization are diametrically opposed to each other, and here is a great example. I started a recent promotion with almost 100 more subscribers but 33 fewer paid subscribers than I added by the end.

During the promotion, I sent three emails to my list offering a paid membership to The Author Stack for 83% off, or $13.60/yr. Those emails converted a small number of readers into paid members, but it also caused 3x more of them to unsubscribe.

When you *grow*, it normally takes *giving something* to find the right people. Meanwhile, *monetization* means *asking something* from those people, which naturally turns away people who don't resonate with your message.

In general, people are *very* okay with taking from you, but get turned off when you ask anything of them. It doesn't matter who you are or how long you've been doing this work, that fact is *always* true.

Everything you do exists on this monetization to growth parallel, and we're always triangulating ourselves on it. I prefer thinking about this in "seasons," where I launch a thing, and then build new subscribers for the next thing.

The growth-to-monetization parallel is a critical balancing act that can determine the success of your writing careers. While growing an audience is essential, it's equally important to plan for sustainable monetization strategies that ensure financial stability. By introducing monetization thoughtfully, focusing on reader experience, and timing the transition carefully, writers can successfully navigate this parallel, achieving both audience growth and a sustainable income. The key is to maintain a balance that supports long-term success, understanding that this journey is ongoing and requires continual adjustments to remain sustainable.

CONTINUITY & SUBSCRIPTIONS

For most authors, success can often feel like a constant hustle. You finish a book, launch it, and watch as the initial surge of sales rolls in. But then what? The reality for many is an exhausting cycle of feast and famine where each book's momentum fades, and the pressure to release another looms overhead. It's an unstable foundation for a business, one that demands an endless supply of creative energy just to keep things afloat.

Continuity shifts this model. Instead of being dependent on one-time book sales, continuity provides an ongoing revenue stream that doesn't vanish the moment a launch is over. With a subscription or membership model, readers commit to an ongoing relationship with an author's work. Whether it's through Patreon, Substack, Ream, or a private membership community, continuity ensures that an author gets paid regularly instead of just when they release something new.

A sustainable author career isn't built on how many books you can crank out in a year. It's built on how many readers stay with you long-term. A one-time book buyer might read your work and move on, but a subscriber? A subscriber is invested. They're returning every month, engaging with your world, and supporting your career in a way that builds momentum over time instead of resetting after every launch.

The financial impact of this model is game-changing. Instead of waking up on the first of every month wondering how many books need to be sold to hit revenue goals, authors with continuity models start with a baseline income they can rely on. Even if they don't release a new book that month, the revenue still comes in. Over time, this removes the constant pressure to release at an unsustainable pace.

There's also an important psychological shift at play. When readers subscribe, they aren't just buying books. They're buying into the author's world. They're making a commitment, whether it's for early access to books, behind-the-scenes content, or exclusive serialized fiction. This level of investment transforms casual readers into superfans, and superfans don't just buy, they advocate. They become part of the marketing engine, sharing their enthusiasm, pulling in new subscribers, and turning an author's business into a self-sustaining ecosystem.

One of the biggest mistakes I see authors make with continuity programs—whether that's Patreon, Ream, Substack, or their own membership—is they add it too late and expect it to immediately carry the weight of their business. They set up a subscription and think, "This will solve everything." But a continuity program isn't a last-minute patch or a magic wand. It's an undercurrent, something that needs time, attention, and gradual momentum before it becomes the reliable foundation you want it to be.

Continuity doesn't work if you throw it together at the moment you feel desperate for stability. If you're relying on it to plug holes in your revenue, it's already too late. Continuity thrives when it's been built into your system early, when every funnel, every launch, and every direct sale you make subtly points readers toward that long-term relationship. The reason these programs work so well for authors with thriving businesses isn't because they're inherently magic—it's because those authors spent years building an audience that trusts them, enjoys being part of their world, and wants to stay connected.

Continuity works best when it's fed by every part of your business. Your book launches, your direct sales, your newsletters, your behind-the-scenes content—all of these elements become small invitations for readers to go deeper. You grow it before you need it, so that when you hit a slower season or want to step back from the constant hustle, that membership base is already strong. It's already delivering dividends, paying out month after month without the stress of starting over.

If you wait until you're exhausted, burned out, and needing quick cash to launch a membership, you're going to be disappointed. It won't scale fast enough. But if you plant those seeds early, nurture them with consistent attention, and treat continuity as part of the long game instead of a quick fix, you'll wake up in a few years with a steady stream of revenue that supports everything you do.

That's what makes it the undercurrent of your business. It's not flashy. It's not loud. But it's there, flowing quietly beneath the surface, carrying you forward when everything else gets noisy and unpredictable.

BUILDING YOUR SUBSCRIPTION WITH INTENTION

When it comes to building continuity into your business, one of the most effective tactics I've seen and used is what I call a PBS-style pledge drive. You know the kind I mean, where the programming keeps rolling, but every so often, they stop to remind you that if you enjoy the content, you can support it directly and get special perks in return. There's no begging or guilt, just a clear reminder that this thing you love continues because people like you help make it possible.

Authors can run their continuity programs in the same way. Instead of constantly pitching your membership and exhausting your readers, you plan strategic, focused campaigns a couple of times a year where you highlight the value of your community and invite readers to join. You show them the behind-the-scenes content they're missing; you talk about what their support allows you to do, and you make it clear that they're part of something bigger.

The key to a good pledge drive is that it's temporary and intentional. For a couple of weeks, you turn up the volume. You talk about your membership in your emails, on social media, in your book backmatter. You feature testimonials from current supporters. You showcase exclusive perks, like early access to books, special editions, bonus content. You might even tie it to a limited-time incentive: join now and get a signed bookplate, a private Q&A, or exclusive merch.

And then, once that window closes, you go back to business as usual. No more heavy promotion, no more constant asks. You've reminded your readers that they can support you, you've given them a clear reason to do so, and then you've left them to make their decision. That's why PBS pledge drives work. They're bursts of focused energy that don't wear out the audience but create moments of collective action.

When done right, a PBS-style pledge drive doesn't just bring in new members, it reinforces your relationship with your readers. It reminds them that they're part of something special, and that their support has real impact. And over time, these drives build momentum, feeding your continuity program so it becomes exactly what it's supposed to be: a stable, growing, quiet force that supports everything else you do.

THE SUBSCRIPTION MODEL IN ACTION

In early 2024, I put this theory to the test. Instead of relying on one-off sales, I ran a series of pledge drives designed to grow my subscription base in short, high-impact bursts. The idea was simple: a limited-time push offering special incentives to get readers to sign up for a monthly membership. I ran four of these pledge drives over the course of the year, tracking how each effort stacked onto the last.

The results were staggering. On January 1st, I had 324 subscribers. By March, after the first pledge drive, that number jumped to 470. By August, it had grown to 789. The next push brought it to 888 by mid-September, and by the end of the year, I had 1,150 paying members in my subscription program.

What's most striking about this growth isn't just the numbers but what they represent. Every single one of those subscribers was contributing monthly revenue to my business, creating an income floor that didn't rely on new releases or retailer promotions. Even if I stopped writing for a few months, the money wouldn't just disappear. This is the power of continuity.

For continuity to work, authors need to move away from thinking about selling books and start thinking about building relationships. The most successful subscription-based authors aren't just churning out content, but creating an ongoing experience. They invite readers into their world, offer them exclusive access, and most importantly, they make their subscribers feel like insiders rather than just customers.

This isn't always an easy transition. Selling a one-off book is transactional. It's simple, clean, and over the moment the reader makes a purchase, but continuity requires trust. It requires showing up consistently, delivering value, and building a connection that keeps readers engaged. That's why many authors hesitate to embrace subscriptions. It feels like a bigger commitment. And it is. But the reward is a business that grows with every passing month, rather than one that resets with every book launch.

If there's one takeaway from this section, it's this: continuity is the key to author freedom. It's what allows authors to step off the hamster wheel of constant launches, unpredictable sales cycles, and algorithm dependencies. It turns a collection of individual book sales into a growing, stable business model that compounds over time. And best of all, it means that instead of chasing new readers every month, authors can focus on deepening their relationship with the ones they already have. That said, since we are building something before you need it, slowly, we also have to think about how to make something that is built to last without burning you out.

HOW TO BUILD SUBSCRIPTION REVENUE THAT LASTS

Once an author understands the power of continuity, the next challenge is making it work. A subscription model isn't just about offering content. It's about building an experience that readers want to stay part of long-term. The difference between a subscription that fizzles out after a few months and one that steadily grows into a six-figure revenue stream comes down to what is offered, how it's structured, and how it's nurtured over time.

That doesn't mean making it flashy. Many authors make the mistake of overcomplicating their subscription models. They feel the need to constantly generate exclusive, never-before-seen content, overwhelming themselves in the process. But the best subscription models aren't built on more work. They're built on repackaging what you're already doing in a way that makes sense for continuity.

A great subscription offers three key things:

1. **Regular Value** – Readers need a reason to stay subscribed. This doesn't mean constant new content; it means something ongoing that makes their subscription feel worthwhile.
2. **Exclusive Access** – Readers who subscribe want to feel like they're getting something others don't. That could be early access to books, behind-the-scenes content, or direct interaction with the author.
3. **A Sense of Belonging** – The best subscription models aren't just about content; they create a community. Readers want to feel like they are part of something special, something built just for them.

The most successful subscription-based authors structure their offerings around what is sustainable, engaging, and valuable. Here's a breakdown of the most effective content types:

1. **Early Access to Books** - One of the easiest and most effective ways to add value to a subscription is by offering early access to upcoming releases. This doesn't require additional work—authors are already writing the books—but it gives subscribers a first look at new material before it's available anywhere else. Readers love being part of something exclusive. By offering them a first read, authors not only provide value but also build anticipation and loyalty. It's a simple but highly effective way to encourage long-term subscriptions.

2. **Serialized Fiction** - Serialized content is one of the strongest drivers of recurring revenue in the author world. Instead of waiting months (or years) for a new book, readers get ongoing installments of a story they're invested in. This keeps them engaged week after week, month after month. Platforms like Substack, Ream, and Patreon make serialization easy by allowing authors to post new chapters on a schedule. Some authors release weekly episodes of a novel-in-progress, while others share bonus side stories that expand their world-building. A well-structured serialized story creates built-in continuity and subscribers won't want to cancel because they need to know what happens next.

3. **Exclusive Behind-the-Scenes Content** - Readers love seeing the creative process unfold. Offering behind-the-scenes insights like character notes, deleted scenes, and author commentary turns the subscription into a deeper experience. This type of content is low effort for authors but highly valuable for readers. It takes what already exists (outlines, rough drafts, world-building notes) and packages it in a way that feels exclusive.

4. **Interactive Experiences** - Subscriptions don't just have to be about content. They can also be about connection. Many authors increase engagement by offering Q&A sessions, live streams, or subscriber-only discussions. This type of direct interaction strengthens the author-reader bond, making readers feel personally connected to the author's success. It's also one of the strongest ways to build reader loyalty—people who feel invested in an author as a person are far less likely to cancel their subscription.

The best way to start a subscription—though most people won't say it this bluntly—is by monetizing your garbage. And I don't mean that in a bad way. I'm talking about all the stuff you've already created that's just sitting there, collecting digital dust: old short stories, character sketches, alternate endings, deleted chapters, behind-the-scenes notes, early drafts, and process posts. This is the creative "burnoff" that naturally happens when you write a book.

Also, it's the stuff you already have and your readers would kill to get. Think about your favorite author. What would you give to get their first draft, editor notes, character bios, or deleted scenes? That's how your own readers would feel, too.

And if you don't believe that you could be somebody's favorite author…why is your name on the book, then?

Most authors think subscriptions have to be built around new, original content every week, and that's what overwhelms them. But really, your readers love the stuff that feels intimate, exclusive, and messy. They want to see the early notes where you tried one ending and went with another. They want to know which characters didn't make the cut. They want the scraps and side dishes because for them, that's part of being on the inside.

So, when you're starting a continuity program, don't pressure yourself to create endless shiny new things. Start by opening the vault. Package up your "garbage" in a way that feels special. Maybe that's a monthly peek into your cut scenes, a blog post about what you wrestled with in edits, or a collection of old short stories that never quite found a home. All that material becomes the foundation of your membership and you didn't have to write a single new word.

Not only does this take the pressure off, but it shows your readers that there's more to your world than what ends up on the shelves. And the funny thing? What feels like scraps to you often feels like treasure to your most loyal fans. So don't overthink it. Start by monetizing the creative leftovers. That's the easiest way to get your subscription rolling and it frees you up to build momentum before you ever worry about creating something new from scratch.

HOW TO GROW A SUBSCRIPTION WITHOUT BURNOUT

A subscription model is only valuable if it's sustainable. Many authors, excited by the prospect of recurring revenue, launch ambitious subscription plans filled with exclusive content, personalized bonuses, and constant engagement promises. But soon, they find themselves overwhelmed, struggling to keep up with the demands of their subscribers. What started as an exciting opportunity quickly becomes a burden, leading to exhaustion and, eventually, subscriber churn.

The key to avoiding burnout while maintaining a thriving subscription lies in three core principles. First, an author should only provide what is easy to maintain. A subscription should not feel like a second job, constantly pulling focus away from writing books. Instead of creating entirely new content from scratch, successful subscription models repurpose existing materials, such as early access to books, behind-the-scenes insights, or extended versions of content already being produced.

Second, the offer should be simple and clear. Readers don't want to wade through a dozen different tiers, each with complicated perks and add-ons. Too many choices create confusion, and confusion reduces sign-ups. The most effective subscriptions have one compelling offer, making it easy for readers to understand exactly what they're getting and why it's worth their money.

Finally, the focus should always be on long-term engagement rather than just acquiring new subscribers. A single reader who stays subscribed for a year is far more valuable than two readers who sign up for a month and leave. Sustainable subscription models prioritize retention over rapid growth, ensuring that subscribers feel like they're part of an ongoing experience rather than just receiving random content. One author, for example, shifted their strategy from constant new content to deeply engaging, community-driven material. The result? Eighty percent of their new subscribers stayed past the critical 90-day mark, proving that engagement, not just volume, is what keeps a subscription alive.

A successful subscription isn't about offering more. It's about offering something meaningful, maintainable, and engaging enough to keep readers coming back month after month.

THE READER JOURNEY: FROM CASUAL BUYER TO SUPERFAN

Once an author has built a subscription model and attracted their first members, the next challenge is keeping them engaged. A subscription isn't just about getting someone to sign up. It's about creating an experience compelling enough that readers want to stay subscribed month after month.

The key to long-term retention is engagement. When readers feel connected to an author's world, they're not just paying for content—they're investing in a relationship. Engaged subscribers don't just stay; they become superfans, advocates, and part of the engine that fuels the long-term sustainability of an author business. When a reader first subscribes, they're excited. They believe in the author's work and want to support it. But without consistent engagement, that initial excitement fades. A subscriber who isn't actively engaged will eventually cancel, not because they dislike the content, but because they don't feel invested anymore.

Keeping subscribers engaged means moving them along a journey, from casual reader to superfan. Superfans aren't just paying for content; they see themselves as part of something bigger. They're proud to be members, actively participate in discussions, and evangelize the author's work to others.

To move readers along this journey, authors need to create ongoing touchpoints that reinforce engagement and deepen their connection to the work.

HOW TO STRUCTURE AN ENGAGING READER COMMUNITY

A thriving subscription model isn't just about delivering content. It's about building an interactive experience. Readers stay subscribed when they feel like they're part of something special.

The most successful subscription-based authors don't just publish and disappear. They create a space where subscribers can interact, discuss, and feel connected to the author's journey. Here's how:

1. **Create a Private Community Space** - A private space, whether it's Facebook, Discord, Substack Chat, or even a dedicated forum, gives subscribers a place to connect with each other and the author. When done right, these communities become self-sustaining, with members keeping discussions alive even when the author isn't active. Instead of just talking at subscribers, community spaces allow them to talk to each other. This increases retention because readers stay for the relationships, not just the content.

2. **Run Exclusive Live Events** - Subscribers stay engaged when they feel seen and valued. Live events like Q&A sessions, behind-the-scenes discussions, or special book readings create interactive moments that strengthen connection. A well-timed live event can re-energize a subscription base, keeping members engaged between major content drops. The best events create a sense of access, making subscribers feel like insiders rather than just customers.

3. **Encourage Reader-Driven Interaction** - The best communities don't revolve entirely around the author. They allow readers to create their own interactions. Successful subscription models encourage subscriber-generated discussions (fan theories, character deep dives), community book clubs or reading challenges, polls and audience-driven content decisions, among others. When a subscription feels interactive, members stay because they're engaged in the experience, not just the content.

THE POWER OF PLEDGE DRIVES FOR SUBSCRIPTION GROWTH

We talked about pledge drives above, but let's dive into them more deeply now. Most subscriptions grow slowly over time, but authors can accelerate that growth through periodic pledge drives. These short, high-impact campaigns are designed to create urgency and drive new memberships in bulk.

A pledge drive is a limited-time membership push that offers special bonuses or exclusive content to encourage sign-ups. Instead of waiting for new subscribers to trickle in, a pledge drive compacts a month's worth of growth into a few days.

A well-structured pledge drive doesn't just drive new sign-ups. It **strengthens the entire subscription ecosystem**. Here's how to set one up for success:

1. TIMING YOUR PLEDGE DRIVES

Most successful subscription-based businesses run 2-4 pledge drives per year, aligning them with big events, book launches, or major content drops. Some of the best times to run pledge drives are:

- **Start of the year** (New Year, new commitments).
- **Mid-year refresh** (June/July boost before summer lulls).
- **Major book launches** (turn new readers into subscribers).
- **Holiday seasons** (end-of-year bonuses).

2. CREATING A LIMITED-TIME OFFER

A pledge drive works only if there's a reason to join now. The best offers include:

- **Exclusive bonus content** (only available to subscribers who join during the drive).
- **Special pricing deals** (discounted first-month rates, lifetime access options).
- **Community perks** (VIP access, name recognition in upcoming projects).

The most important element? The deal must not be available outside the pledge drive. Readers need to know this is their best chance to subscribe.

3. PROMOTING THE PLEDGE DRIVE

A pledge drive should feel like an event, not just another promotion. The key to success is building momentum before the drive begins.

- **Week before:** Announce the upcoming pledge drive, tease the bonuses.
- **3 days before:** Increase hype with subscriber testimonials and exclusive previews.
- **Launch day:** Go all-in with emails, live Q&As, and social media engagement.
- **Final push:** Countdown reminders create urgency before the drive ends.

By structuring pledge drives this way, authors can quickly scale their subscriptions while reinforcing engagement.

HOW RECURRING REVENUE CHANGES AN AUTHOR'S BUSINESS

A subscription model isn't just about keeping readers engaged. It's about building a financial foundation that allows an author to create freely, without the stress of unpredictable income spikes. While most authors rely on launch cycles and retailer promotions for revenue, a continuity model provides predictable, recurring income that grows over time.

The difference between an author who feels like they're always chasing the next sale and an author who can plan long-term comes down to how much of their income is stable and recurring. When revenue is consistent month to month, authors can take bigger creative risks, focus on higher-quality projects, and scale their businesses without burnout.

Most authors wake up at the beginning of each month with one thought: *"How many books do I need to sell this month to pay my bills?"* The unpredictability of retail sales makes it difficult to plan ahead. But when subscriptions provide a reliable baseline income, everything changes.

Instead of starting at zero each month, an author with a strong subscription base begins with money already in the bank. Even if they don't release a new book or run a major promotion, their subscribers continue to support them.

This shift has a profound impact on an author's business, transforming the way they approach both their finances and their creative work. It really is like having a job, because you get paid regularly instead of in chaotic spurts, which is nice for lots of authors, myself included. I only make about $2k/month from my subscription but it pays my mortgage every month, which isn't nothing, either.

Without the constant pressure to release new books just to maintain income, authors can step away from the relentless production cycle that often leads to burnout. Instead of feeling trapped in an endless loop of rapid-fire publishing, they gain the freedom to pace their releases strategically, focusing on quality rather than just speed.

With that stability, financial planning becomes far more predictable. Rather than relying on fluctuating book sales and uncertain royalties, a steady stream of subscription revenue allows authors to plan ahead with confidence. They can invest in hiring help, running ads, and funding future projects without the stress of waiting for retailer payouts or wondering if their next launch will succeed. Knowing that a certain amount of revenue will arrive each month provides a level of financial security that is often missing from retail-only models.

Perhaps the most significant shift is in creative freedom. When financial survival is no longer dependent on chasing trends or constantly producing what the market demands, authors can take risks. They can write passion projects, explore new genres, or experiment with unique formats without the fear that doing so will derail their income. This kind of security is what allows authors to build lasting, meaningful careers instead of constantly chasing the next quick win.

In essence, continuity is the foundation of financial independence for authors. It removes the instability of retail-based sales and replaces it with a stable, scalable revenue model that allows for long-term success. Instead of living launch to launch, authors who embrace continuity build a business that sustains itself, freeing them to focus on what they do best: writing.

HOW TO PRICE A SUBSCRIPTION FOR MAXIMUM RETENTION

One of the biggest mistakes authors make with subscriptions is pricing them incorrectly, either too high, which prevents people from joining, or too low, which devalues the offering and makes it unsustainable.

A successful subscription model balances affordability with long-term retention. Readers should feel like they're getting value far beyond the cost, but the price must also support the author's time and effort.

PROVEN PRICING STRATEGIES FOR AUTHOR SUBSCRIPTIONS

Most successful subscription models follow some variation of a **three-tier structure**, which allows readers to choose the level that fits them best.

- **Basic Tier ($5/month)** – Ideal for casual readers who want early access to books, exclusive updates, and community membership.
- **Premium Tier ($15/month)** – The most popular tier, offering everything in Basic, plus serialized fiction, behind-the-scenes content, and deeper engagement.

- **VIP Tier ($50+/month)** – Designed for superfans who want **direct interaction**, such as private Q&As, signed books, or even coaching/mentorship.

Most subscribers will choose the middle tier, making it the core of the model. VIP tiers appeal to superfans and can bring in a significant amount of additional revenue without requiring a large number of subscribers. If you use Substack, you can use your Founding tier as your VIP tier, but then you only get one other tier. I know people complain about it, but I actually prefer starting with just one tier, that is very easy on you, where all people get is stuff you already have, and then you can grow it over time as you find out what your audience wants.

While the monthly fee provides stable income, the most successful subscription-based authors go beyond just the subscription fee to maximize revenue per subscriber.

1. UPSELLS & EXCLUSIVE OFFERS

Subscribers are already invested in the author's world, making them far more likely to purchase additional content. Many subscription-based authors offer special, subscriber-only sales on exclusive editions, bundles, or merchandise.

For example, an author might:

- Offer **signed special editions** of books, only available to subscribers.
- Give **VIP members first access** to limited time offers before the general public.
- Create **annual or lifetime membership options**, allowing fans to lock in benefits at a higher upfront price.

2. ANNUAL SUBSCRIPTIONS FOR HIGHER RETENTION

Many readers are hesitant to commit to monthly payments but are willing to pay once a year to avoid ongoing charges. Offering an annual membership option at a discounted rate can lock in revenue upfront while improving retention.

For example, instead of paying $15/month, a reader might opt for a $150/year plan (essentially getting two months free). This provides predictable income for the author while reducing churn.

3. RUNNING SPECIAL MEMBER-ONLY PROMOTIONS

Subscription members love exclusivity, so offering subscriber-only discounts, sales, or limited-time rewards is a great way to increase engagement and revenue.

Successful subscription-based authors frequently:

- Offer holiday sales where subscribers get extra bonuses or discounts.
- Give exclusive Kickstarter perks to members who stay subscribed through a launch.
- Provide early access to paid courses, workshops, or signed book bundles.

This not only adds value to the subscription but also reinforces why subscribers should stay long-term.

HOW TO REDUCE SUBSCRIBER CHURN (PREVENTING MEMBERSHIP DROP-OFFS)

While growing a subscription base is essential, keeping existing members engaged is just as important. Many authors celebrate sign-ups but fail to track churn, which is the rate at which subscribers cancel their memberships. If churn is too high, even a fast-growing subscription base will stagnate or shrink over time.

Churn is a natural part of any subscription business, but the goal is to reduce it as much as possible by ensuring that subscribers remain engaged, feel valued, and continue seeing the worth of their membership. Here are the three biggest reasons for subscriber churn.

1. **Lack of Ongoing Engagement**
   Readers sign up because they're excited about **exclusive content**, but if they stop engaging, they're more likely to cancel.
   a. **Solution:** Implement **consistent touchpoints** such as monthly Q&As, polls, and personalized check-ins. Encourage participation **in community spaces** so readers stay invested.
2. **Unclear Value Over Time**
   Readers need to feel like they are continuously getting **something they can't get elsewhere**. If the subscription becomes stagnant, they will start questioning its value.
   a. **Solution:** Introduce **periodic subscriber-only events**, surprise bonuses, or exclusive sneak peeks at future work. Keep them excited about what's next.
3. **Financial Drop-Offs & Subscription Fatigue**
   Sometimes, readers cancel for financial reasons, or they feel like they're "stacking too many subscriptions."
   a. **Solution:** Offer **tiered pricing** so subscribers can **downgrade instead of canceling completely**. Many will prefer to **stay on at a lower tier** rather than leaving entirely.

Even with great engagement, some level of churn is inevitable, so the best strategy is to counteract it by re-engaging members before they leave. Here's how:

- **Win-Back Campaigns:** If a subscriber cancels, trigger an automated email sequence offering them a special incentive to rejoin.
- **Exit Surveys:** When someone cancels, ask why. Then use that feedback to improve the subscription.
- **Subscriber Recognition:** Call out engaged members publicly, feature their comments, and make them feel valued.
- **Exclusive "Loyalty Perks" for Long-Term Members:** Offering a six-month or one-year milestone reward encourages long-term retention.

Churn isn't just about numbers. It's about understanding why people leave and making changes that increase long-term retention. The more effort put into keeping readers engaged, the less work is required to constantly find new subscribers.

HOW TO INTEGRATE SUBSCRIPTION & COMMUNITY INTO A FULL AUTHOR ECOSYSTEM

For a subscription model to be sustainable, it needs to fit alongside direct sales, Kickstarter, and retailer strategies rather than feeling like a completely separate project. When continuity is built into an existing ecosystem, it becomes an easy-to-maintain revenue stream instead of an ongoing burden.

Instead of trying to "sell" subscriptions on their own, successful authors funnel readers from other platforms into their memberships organically. This means:

- Using Kickstarter backers as the first pool of subscribers by offering ongoing perks for continued membership.
- Encouraging retailer readers to join the subscription via book backmatter and exclusive offers.
- Using direct sales to drive recurring revenue. Once someone buys from an author's webstore, offering them a membership becomes a natural next step.

The key is making subscription an extension of the reader's journey, rather than something separate they have to seek out. Many authors hesitate to embrace continuity because they fear the workload, struggle with retention, or aren't sure how to promote it. But these challenges can be mitigated with the right approach.

1. "I DON'T HAVE TIME TO RUN A SUBSCRIPTION"

A common misconception is that a membership model requires constant new content creation. But the most successful authors don't create extra work. They repurpose what they're already doing.

- **Use early drafts, character notes, and deleted scenes as exclusive content.**
- **Offer early access to books and serialized fiction that you're already writing.**
- **Use "burn-off" content**—material you create naturally in your writing process—rather than trying to invent new content from scratch.

2. "SUBSCRIBERS KEEP LEAVING AFTER A FEW MONTHS"

Retention is **just as important as attracting new subscribers**. Authors need to **give readers a reason to stay** beyond the initial excitement.

- Introduce **milestone rewards**—subscribers who stay for 6+ months get a special bonus.
- Offer **tiered pricing** so that readers who are considering canceling can downgrade instead.
- Keep engagement **fresh with periodic pledge drives, subscriber-only events, and exclusive sneak peeks.**

3. "I DON'T KNOW HOW TO MARKET MY SUBSCRIPTION"

Many authors struggle with **how to sell** a membership. The key isn't to treat it like a hard sell—it's to make it **a natural part of the reader's journey**.

- **Tie it into other marketing efforts.** Instead of promoting a membership outright, **mention it in the context of an exclusive perk or bonus.**
- **Use testimonials from current members** to show the value of subscribing.
- **Leverage scarcity**, offer limited time sign-up bonuses for new members.

The more effortlessly a subscription fits into an author's overall strategy, the easier it is to sell

AUTOMATING SUBSCRIPTION GROWTH FOR LONG-TERM SUCCESS

Once a continuity model is set up, the goal is to make it run with as little manual effort as possible. Many authors struggle with subscriptions because they feel like they need to actively manage them every day, but successful memberships are built on automated systems that sustain themselves.

1. EMAIL SEQUENCES THAT SELL THE SUBSCRIPTION AUTOMATICALLY

Instead of constantly trying to convince new subscribers to join, authors can create **pre-written email sequences** that drive membership growth.

For example:

- A reader downloads a free book → They get an email sequence introducing the subscription.
- A Kickstarter backer receives exclusive rewards → An email sequence invites them to join for ongoing benefits.
- A webstore buyer makes a purchase → They're offered a **limited-time subscription discount**.

This ensures that new potential subscribers are always entering the funnel, even if the author isn't actively promoting it.

2. RECURRING PLEDGE DRIVES THAT RUN ON A SCHEDULE

Pledge drives don't need to be manually created each time. They can be **built into a yearly promotional calendar**.

- **January** – New Year sign-up push ("Start the year with exclusive early access to my 2024 releases").
- **June** – Mid-year subscriber boost ("Summer reading club: Join now for a special members-only book").
- **October** – Holiday pledge drive ("Sign up now and get early access to my end-of-year special edition").

By structuring pledge drives into the calendar in advance, subscription growth becomes predictable and scalable.

3. COMMUNITY ENGAGEMENT THAT RUNS ITSELF

Many authors assume that they need to personally engage with subscribers every day to keep retention high. But strong communities sustain themselves when built correctly. Instead of trying to be active in a community all the time, successful authors:

- **Designate moderators or community managers** to run discussions.
- **Create discussion prompts and let subscribers take the lead.**
- **Offer occasional live events** but let subscribers build their own engagement in between.

By setting the right foundation, a subscription community runs itself over time.

4. USING AI AND ZAPIER TO TAKE IT EVEN FURTHER

This is where things get fun. With tools like Zapier and Make, you can connect all your platforms so that when someone joins your newsletter, gets tagged as a Kickstarter backer, or buys from your store, they're automatically tagged, segmented, and entered into the right sequences without you ever touching it. No manual importing. No chasing down spreadsheets. Just smooth, behind-the-scenes automation.

And with AI tools, you can take content creation pressure off yourself. AI can help draft social posts, brainstorm community prompts, or even outline bonus content ideas that you can quickly polish and make your own. You're still the creative force, but AI lets you scale without doubling your workload. Subscription platforms like Mighty and Circle even have AI agents to help you even more.

When you put all of this together—smart automations, scheduled pledge drives, communities that thrive on their own, and the strategic use of AI—you create a subscription system that grows quietly and predictably in the background, paying off month after month, year after year.

WHY CONTINUITY SHOULD BE EVERY AUTHOR'S GOAL

Subscription models aren't just another income stream, they are the key to financial stability in an unpredictable industry. Unlike retailer sales, which fluctuate based on algorithms, ad costs, and market trends, a subscription creates consistent, recurring revenue that an author can rely on. Instead of constantly chasing the next launch to generate income, authors who embrace continuity can predict their monthly revenue, allowing them to plan projects, invest in their business, and write without financial pressure.

This shift reduces stress in ways that many authors don't realize until they experience it firsthand. Retail platforms control visibility, pricing, and recommendations, often leaving authors feeling powerless when their sales drop unexpectedly, but with a strong subscription model, an author's income is no longer tied to the whims of retailer algorithms. With one, they own their revenue and that means more creative control, more financial independence, and less worry about external factors beyond their control.

Beyond financial benefits, a subscription also deepens the relationship between authors and readers. Instead of casual fans who buy a book and move on, subscribers become long-term superfans, committed to the author's work. These readers are invested in the journey, eager for new releases, and far more likely to support future projects. The relationship shifts from transactional to ongoing engagement, turning one-time buyers into a dedicated, recurring audience.

The best part? A subscription compounds over time. What starts with a few dozen members can grow into hundreds or even thousands of paying supporters, creating a revenue foundation that no longer depends on constant book launches. With every new book, every new marketing push, and every new reader who enters the ecosystem, the subscription model grows stronger.

For authors looking to future-proof their careers, continuity isn't just a smart option, it's the best path forward. A stable, recurring income allows authors to take creative risks, focus on passion projects, and build a business that supports them for years to come. Instead of being trapped in a cycle of unpredictable launches, they create a sustainable, scalable system that works even when they aren't actively promoting.

THE CASUAL READER RETAILER FUNNEL

Most authors see retailers like Amazon, Kobo, Apple Books, and Barnes & Noble as the final step in their sales strategy. They focus on ranking high in algorithms, optimizing their metadata, and chasing bestseller status thinking that once their book is available, success will come from hitting the right lists or landing a big promotion.

But this is a fundamentally flawed approach to long-term success. Retailers aren't the end goal; they're the starting point. They are reader acquisition tools, not the place where an author builds a thriving, sustainable business. In an integrated author ecosystem, the real power of retailers isn't in how many books they sell. It's in how many readers they introduce to an author's world.

Authors who build their business exclusively around retailer sales are placing their success in the hands of ever-changing algorithms and unpredictable market forces. What works one year may fail the next.

Retailers control pricing, visibility, and promotional opportunities, which means authors relying entirely on these platforms are at their mercy. Algorithms change, ad costs rise, and bestseller lists become harder to crack. If an author doesn't have a direct relationship with their readers, they risk losing everything when retailers shift their priorities.

This is why the most successful authors don't stop at selling books on Amazon. They use retailers to find their readers, then funnel them into their own ecosystem, where they have control over sales, pricing, and engagement.

Instead of seeing an Amazon sale as the ultimate goal, authors should ask a better question, namely *"How can I use this retailer sale to build a long-term reader relationship?"*

Every book sold on a retailer should be seen as the *beginning* of a reader's journey, not the *end*. Too many authors focus solely on making the sale, assuming that if a reader enjoys the book, they'll naturally return for more. The reality is that without a clear next step, most readers will finish a book and move on, either to another author or to whatever else catches their attention.

The real opportunity in retailer sales isn't just the royalty from that first purchase. It's what happens next. The goal should always be to capture that reader's interest and guide them toward deeper engagement. That might mean directing them to an email list, where they'll receive updates about new books, exclusive content, and special offers. Once an author has a reader's email, they have a direct line of communication—no longer relying on Amazon's algorithm to put their next release in front of them.

For authors using subscription models, retailer readers can be encouraged to go beyond one-time purchases and instead become ongoing supporters. A reader who enjoyed a book on Amazon might be willing to pay for early access to future releases, bonus stories, or behind-the-scenes content. By offering them an easy way to upgrade their experience through a subscription, authors create long-term relationships instead of fleeting transactions.

Another key transition is moving retailer readers into direct sales, where the author keeps more of the profit and has full control over pricing, bundling, and promotions. If a reader has already enjoyed a book, offering them an exclusive signed edition, audiobook bundle, or special hardcover through a webstore makes it more likely they'll buy direct in the future.

Retailer sales are just the first interaction with a reader. What happens next determines whether that reader remains a casual buyer or becomes a long-term, high-value customer. Authors who master this transition don't just sell books, they build engaged, loyal audiences that support their work for years to come.

RETAILERS AS LEAD GENERATORS FOR DIRECT SALES & SUBSCRIPTIONS

The best way to think about retailer platforms is like a giant, automated lead-generation machine. Millions of readers browse Amazon, Kobo, and Apple Books every day, and an author's goal should be to leverage this traffic to find their ideal audience, then move those readers into direct engagement channels.

Instead of treating retailer buyers as one-time customers, authors should design a system that captures, nurtures, and converts them into long-term supporters.

This means:

1. **Optimizing Book Backmatter to Drive Readers to an Email List**
   a. Every book should include a **compelling, high-value call to action** directing readers to a

    landing page for a free bonus, exclusive content, or a discount.

    b. The goal isn't just to get them on a list. It's to make them **excited to join** the author's ecosystem.

2. **Using Pre-orders & First-in-Series Promotions to Capture More Readers**

    a. A well-priced first-in-series book attracts casual readers who might not have heard of the author before.

    b. Running retailer promotions on Book 1 ensures ongoing audience growth, while backmatter and email funnels move them into deeper engagement.

3. **Positioning Retailer Sales to Create Lifetime Customers**

    a. Instead of pushing every book separately, authors should guide readers through a structured journey that leads them to direct purchases and ongoing engagement.

    b. This means using email sequences, automated offers, and subscriber perks to make sure a casual buyer doesn't just stop after one book.

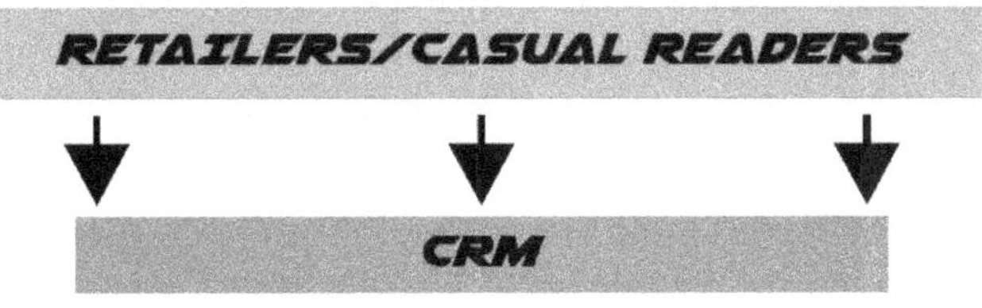

THE CASUAL READER FUNNEL—HOW RETAILERS FIT INTO A LARGER AUTHOR ECOSYSTEM

Selling books on Amazon, Kobo, and Apple Books is easy. Keeping those readers engaged for the long term? That's the real challenge. Most readers who buy a book on a retailer will never interact with the author again, not because they didn't enjoy the book, but because there was no system in place to keep them connected.

This is where the casual reader funnel comes into play.

Retailers attract a wide range of readers, from those casually browsing for a new book to die-hard genre fans searching for their next binge-worthy series. But not all of them will naturally stick around. A funnel ensures that once a reader finds an author's book, they are guided toward deeper engagement, whether that's joining an email list, subscribing to a membership, or buying direct from the author.

This section will break down how to convert one-time retailer buyers into long-term, engaged fans by structuring a reader funnel that leads them from a single book purchase to ongoing direct engagement.

As we already learned, a funnel is a structured path that moves readers from one level of engagement to the next. At the top, retailers expose books to a large pool of potential readers. But without a system in place, those readers will never take another action beyond buying the book.

A well-built casual reader funnel ensures that:

1. Retailers introduce the reader to the author's work.
2. A compelling backmatter call-to-action leads them to take the next step.
3. Email automation, bonus content, and exclusive offers keep them engaged.
4. Readers who love the experience move into direct sales, subscriptions, and higher-value purchases.

Every successful direct-selling author uses a version of this system, even if they primarily sell on retailers.

OPTIMIZING BOOK BACKMATTER TO CAPTURE READERS

One of the biggest missed opportunities in the author ecosystem is underutilized backmatter, which the section directly after the end of a book that guides readers to take action after they finish reading.

Most authors make a critical mistake at the end of their books by failing to guide the reader toward the next step. Some do nothing at all, letting the book simply end with no invitation to continue the journey. Others list all their other books, hoping that sheer volume will entice the reader to buy another, but without a clear direction, many readers simply move on. Then there are those who include a generic "sign up for my newsletter" link, which, without a compelling reason, rarely motivates action.

The most successful authors treat the end of their book as a strategic conversion point. Instead of leaving the reader's next step up to chance, they design a clear, irresistible call to action that moves the reader deeper into their ecosystem. This could mean inviting them to download an exclusive bonus chapter in exchange for their email, offering a discount on a direct sales bundle, or leading them into a subscription where they can access early releases and exclusive content.

A reader who reaches the end of a book is already engaged. After all, they've spent hours immersed in the author's world. This is the perfect moment to capture their interest and guide them toward deeper engagement. When authors optimize this transition, they don't just sell one book. They build long-term relationships with readers who continue to buy, support, and advocate for their work.

The most successful authors treat the end of their book like a strategic conversion point.

Instead of just hoping readers will find another book, they actively guide them to the next step. The key to high-converting backmatter is giving readers a clear, enticing reason to take action right away. This means:

1. A strong, direct headline – "Want More Exclusive Stories? Get a Free Bonus Chapter Here!"
2. A reason to act now – "This is only available for a limited time."
3. A simple call-to-action – A direct link to an email opt-in page, not just a website homepage.

For example:

Thank you for reading! If you enjoyed this book, I've got a special bonus story that expands on what happens next! It's only available to my VIP readers, and you can grab it here:

→ Click here to get your free bonus now!

This subtle shift in language makes the difference between a reader who moves on after finishing the book and one who actively engages with the author's ecosystem.

USING FIRST-IN-SERIES PROMOTIONS TO HOOK NEW READERS

One of the best ways to bring in new readers at scale is through first-in-series promotions. This isn't a new concept, but what matters is how strategically you use it. Offering the first book of a series at a discounted price or even free isn't about giving away your work for nothing. It's about creating an on-ramp into your world that feels easy, low-risk, and exciting for new readers.

The key here is to stop thinking about that first book as a standalone profit center. It's not where the money is. The value of that first book is in its ability to turn curious strangers into long-term readers who will follow you through multiple books, back your crowdfunding campaigns, join your subscription programs, and buy special editions down the line.

Many of the most successful direct-selling authors don't flinch at giving away that first book, or deeply discounting it, because they understand the math. The goal isn't to squeeze a few bucks out of one sale. The goal is to capture attention at scale and funnel those readers into your ecosystem, where they can become part of your flywheel.

When done right, first-in-series promotions become one of your most powerful growth tools. You're lowering the barrier to entry and maximizing discoverability, but you're doing it with a plan. You're not just tossing free books into the void. You're sending readers to your direct store, capturing their email, and starting a relationship.

And that relationship pays dividends far beyond what a single $4.99 sale ever could. A reader who takes a chance on a discounted or free book, loves it, and is then guided into your world can become a customer who buys every book you write for years to come. They might become part of your membership, they might support your Kickstarter, they might join your community. But none of that happens if you aren't willing to open the door with that first book.

It's a long game. And the authors who lean into it are the ones who see their readership compound over time. They're not relying on quick hits. They're building something durable, scalable, and profitable for the long haul.

PRE-ORDERS & EXCLUSIVE CONTENT AS A FUNNEL ACCELERATOR

Retailers also offer pre-orders as one of the most powerful tools for reader acquisition and retention. Pre-orders aren't just about generating early sales. They're about keeping readers in your world between releases. Every author knows that moment of panic after a reader finishes a book: will they stick around for the next one, or will they drift off to someone else's work? A well-placed pre-order is the answer to that question.

When you have your next book's pre-order linked in the backmatter, you're essentially handing readers a roadmap that says, *"You enjoyed this? Great. Here's what's next."* Instead of leaving them to wander the digital shelves in search of their next read, you're offering them a direct pathway back into your story world. This simple move prevents reader drop-off, keeping the momentum alive while anticipation builds for your next release.

But pre-orders aren't just about convenience. They're also a tool for community engagement and exclusivity. When you offer pre-order bonuses like early chapters, special short stories, or exclusive behind-the-scenes content, you're giving readers a reason to stay connected. Your most loyal fans will jump at the chance to get early access or bonus material that nobody else sees. This doesn't just drive pre-order numbers. It reinforces the idea that being part of your ecosystem comes with privileges.

For subscription members or those on your email list, pre-orders become even more powerful. You can position them as insider perks, making your subscribers the first to know, the first to order, and the first to receive exclusive rewards. This kind of treatment doesn't just drive conversions, but it also deepens loyalty. Readers feel like they're part of something special, and that sense of exclusivity makes them more likely to stick around for the long haul.

Retailers themselves reward strong pre-order activity. Early sales signals tell the algorithm that your book is worth paying attention to. As those numbers grow, your pre-order can climb sales charts, appear in recommendation carousels, and generate organic visibility that would otherwise cost you hundreds or thousands in ad spend. By the time your book officially launches, you're not starting from zero. You're building on months of momentum, which makes every launch more powerful and profitable.

At its core, a pre-order isn't just a placeholder. It's a bridge between books, one that guides readers from their last reading experience straight into the anticipation of the next. It keeps your audience engaged, maintains retailer relevance, and sets up your launches to succeed before the book ever hits virtual shelves. Smart authors treat pre-orders as part of their long-term reader strategy, not as a last-minute checkbox. Because when done right, pre-orders don't just sell the next book. They keep readers excited, engaged, and firmly planted in your world.

WHY RETAILER PROMOTIONS ARE A LONG-TERM PLAY, NOT A SHORT-TERM WIN

Many authors chase promotional success on retailers without having a structured funnel in place. They run a BookBub Featured Deal, a Kindle Countdown, or a Kobo promotion and celebrate the temporary spike in sales.

But without a system that captures those readers and moves them into long-term engagement, that traffic disappears.

Instead of treating retailer promotions as isolated, one-time events, successful authors use them as strategic entry points into their larger ecosystem. A well-executed promotion isn't just about generating a temporary sales spike, it's an opportunity to capture new readers, guide them into deeper engagement, and turn them into long-term customers.

One of the most effective ways to do this is by ensuring that every promotion leads somewhere meaningful. Instead of just discounting a book and hoping for future sales, authors should use retailer promotions to funnel readers toward backmatter opt-ins and exclusive offers. A reader who picks up a discounted ebook is already interested in the author's work. This is the perfect moment to invite them to claim a bonus story, an exclusive discount on a web store bundle, or early access to a new release.

Beyond the initial promotion, authors who automate their follow-up sequences are able to nurture these readers into repeat buyers. When a new reader joins an email list through a promotion, they shouldn't just receive a generic welcome email. They should be guided through a sequence that introduces them to the author's world, showcases additional books, and presents opportunities to buy directly. A well-structured follow-up ensures that the reader's journey doesn't end with a single discounted purchase, it continues into subscriptions, special editions, or web store sales.

Tracking conversion rates is just as important as running the promotion itself. Instead of simply looking at how many books were sold, authors who measure how many readers transition from retailer promotions into direct engagement gain a clearer picture of their true long-term value. If a BookBub deal leads to thousands of downloads but few email sign-ups or direct sales, it may not be as successful as an author initially believes. But if even a small percentage of those discounted buyers convert into superfans who regularly buy premium products or join a subscription, the promotion has done its job.

When done correctly, a single retailer promotion isn't just a way to boost rankings or generate short-term revenue. It's a catalyst for long-term engagement. The authors who understand this don't just sell books during a promotion, they build a base of loyal readers who continue to support them for years to come.

HOW RETAILER SALES FUEL THE ENTIRE ECOSYSTEM

Retailer platforms like Amazon, Kobo, Apple Books, and Google Play are powered by algorithms. While many authors see these algorithms as unpredictable or even frustrating, those who understand how to work with them instead of against them can turn retailer sales into a powerful engine that fuels their entire business, including direct sales, subscriptions, and crowdfunding campaigns.

Retailer algorithms don't exist in isolation. The success of a book on Amazon, for example, often has a ripple effect on everything else an author does. A spike in retailer sales can drive up Kickstarter visibility, increase direct store traffic, and even boost long-term subscriber retention.

This section will explore how retail sales momentum impacts an author's entire ecosystem, how to position books for algorithmic success, and how to use retailer promotions to create a spillover effect that benefits every part of an author's business.

HOW A SPIKE IN RETAILER SALES BOOSTS THE ENTIRE ECOSYSTEM

When a book **sells well on a retailer**, it doesn't just result in higher royalties. It triggers algorithmic signals that amplify an author's entire platform.

Here's what happens when a book starts gaining traction:

1. **Increased Discoverability on the Retailer**
   a. When a book sells well, it **ranks higher in search results and category lists**.
   b. It starts appearing in **"Also Boughts" and recommendation engines**, leading to organic visibility.
2. **Greater External Visibility**
   a. Readers who buy on Amazon or Kobo **start discussing the book online**, increasing social proof.
   b. Retailer momentum often leads to **higher traffic on an author's website and direct store**.
3. **A Spillover Effect into Kickstarter & Subscriptions**
   a. A well-performing book creates **brand awareness**, making readers **more likely to support future crowdfunding campaigns**.

b.   Authors who **capture retailer buyers via backmatter links** see a **steady increase in subscriber numbers**.

One of the biggest misconceptions authors have is that retailer sales are just about launch spikes. But algorithms don't just look at how many books were sold. They measure how engaged readers are over time.

If a book has consistent sales, high readthrough (for KU authors), and strong engagement, the retailer will keep promoting it long after the initial launch. Retailers want money, because of capitalism, and are incentivized to sell books that sell so they make more money. They are agnostic to what they are selling (with few exceptions), as long as it sells.

Retailer algorithms are designed to prioritize books that continue generating sales, engagement, and reader activity over time. Many authors focus on short-term promotions, believing that a single sales spike will push their book into visibility, but without a sustained strategy, those gains quickly disappear. The books that perform well long-term on Amazon, Kobo, and other retailer platforms do so because they consistently signal value to the algorithm.

The first and most important factor is sales consistency. A sudden burst of sales followed by a crash tells the retailer's system that interest in the book was temporary, often leading to a sharp drop in visibility once the promotion ends. On the other hand, books that experience steady, sustained growth are far more valuable to the algorithm. A book that sells 50 copies per day for a month is far more likely to maintain ranking and organic recommendations than a book that sells 1,500 copies in a single day and then nothing for weeks. This is why rolling promotions, staggered ad campaigns, and regular marketing efforts are more effective than a single, all-or-nothing launch push.

For authors enrolled in Kindle Unlimited, readthrough and page reads play a critical role in visibility. Amazon rewards books that not only get downloaded but also keep readers engaged for long periods. A book that has high page reads, strong readthrough to later books in the series, and low dropout rates signals to Amazon that it is providing value to readers. This leads to higher placement in recommendations, organic visibility in search results, and greater exposure in the Kindle Unlimited ecosystem. Authors who focus on driving series readthrough rather than just selling individual books are more likely to maintain retailer visibility for extended periods.

Another key factor is reader engagement, which includes reviews, ratings, and "Also Bought" connections. Books that receive consistent reviews over time are far more likely to remain in front of potential buyers. This doesn't mean chasing hundreds of reviews immediately after launch, but ensuring a steady trickle of reader feedback, which signals ongoing interest. The "Also Bought" section plays a critical role as well; when an author's book starts appearing in the "Also Boughts" of similar books in their genre, they gain free, organic exposure to new readers. This effect compounds over time, placing their book in front of buyers who are already proven to be interested in similar titles a major advantage that doesn't require ad spend.

Authors who understand sales consistency, reader engagement, and readthrough rates can position their books for long-term success instead of short-term spikes. Instead of seeing each book launch as an isolated event, they structure their marketing to sustain visibility, maintain engagement, and leverage retailer algorithms to their advantage. The result is a self-sustaining book ecosystem that continues driving sales long after launch day has passed.

ADVANCED RETAILER SALES STRATEGIES TO FUNNEL READERS INTO DIRECT ENGAGEMENT

Retailers are great for discoverability and lead generation, but their real power comes from how well an author can use them to convert casual readers into engaged fans. Simply selling books on Amazon or Kobo isn't enough; authors need to design their retailer listings strategically so that readers don't just buy one book and move on. Instead, retailer sales should serve as a gateway that leads readers into email lists, subscriptions, direct sales, and deeper engagement.

This section will break down how to structure book listings, optimize metadata, and use promotional strategies to ensure that retailer sales aren't just one-off transactions, but part of a long-term engagement funnel.

Many authors focus solely on selling individual books, but the real value lies in getting readers to continue through a series. Instead of thinking about how to sell one book at a time, authors should structure their retailer presence so that each book leads naturally into the next step of the reader journey.

1. FIRST-IN-SERIES PRICING & PERMAFREE STRATEGIES

One of the most effective strategies for maximizing long-term engagement from retailer buyers is to offer a low-cost or free entry point into a series.

- Pricing **Book 1 at $0.99 or free** encourages casual readers to try the series.
- Higher-priced books later in the series ensure that engaged readers continue through the funnel.
- Backmatter in Book 1 leads **not just to Book 2, but also to an email list or direct sales offer**.

This creates a structured reader journey, where every retailer sale becomes the first step toward a much larger, long-term relationship.

2. OPTIMIZING READTHROUGH WITH A SERIES FUNNEL

For authors who write series, each book needs to serve a purpose within the funnel.

- **Books 1-3 should be strategically priced** to maximize readthrough, not just short-term revenue.
- **Every book should have clear backmatter calls-to-action** leading to the next book or direct engagement.
- **Box sets and bundles should be positioned as the best value for engaged readers**, keeping them invested in the author's world.

THE IMPORTANCE OF METADATA, KEYWORDS, AND CATEGORY SELECTION

Retailers operate on search-driven discovery systems, meaning that how a book is positioned in metadata and categories directly affects who sees it and how often it gets recommended.

Instead of just uploading a book and hoping it finds the right audience, authors should carefully optimize keywords, categories, and descriptions to increase visibility.

1. CHOOSING THE RIGHT CATEGORIES FOR LONG-TERM DISCOVERABILITY

Amazon allows books to be placed in multiple categories, but many authors choose categories based on competition rather than longevity.

A strong retailer strategy involves:

- **Placing books in categories with steady reader demand** (rather than just chasing trends).
- **Using niche subcategories** that allow books to rank higher with fewer sales.
- **Regularly testing and adjusting categories** to ensure maximum exposure.

2. USING KEYWORDS TO TARGET THE RIGHT READERS

Retailers operate like search engines, meaning that keywords play a massive role in discoverability. A well-optimized book listing should:

- **Use high-traffic, low-competition keywords** to increase organic reach.
- **Mirror search patterns of real readers**, ensuring that people searching for books **find exactly what they're looking for**.
- **Test different keyword strategies** over time to improve performance.

CRAFTING BOOK DESCRIPTIONS THAT CONVERT CASUAL BROWSERS INTO BUYERS

Writing an effective blurb can feel overwhelming, but having multiple approaches in your toolkit makes the task more manageable. Let's explore ***three distinct methods*** for crafting blurbs that grab readers' attention and drive sales.

The Story Core Method approach, developed by Libbie Hawker, breaks your story down to its essential elements:

1. Identify your main character
2. Define what they want
3. Establish what prevents them from getting it
4. Show how they struggle against this force
5. Hint at whether they succeed or fail

Using *The Matrix* as an example: "Neo, a computer programmer, wants to understand the truth about reality. The machines controlling humanity prevent him from breaking free. When a mysterious group offers him the chance to see the truth, Neo must risk everything to fight against the system - if he can survive becoming humanity's last hope."

This method works particularly well for character-driven stories where the protagonist's journey is central to the narrative.

The ***Three-Hook Structure*** approach uses a series of escalating hooks followed by deeper context:

1. Open with three ultra-short descriptions (3-6 words each)
2. Follow with 1-2 paragraphs expanding on the core conflict

3. Include who will love the book
4. End with a call to action

For *The Matrix*: "Reality is a lie. Humanity sleeps in chains. One man can wake us all.

Thomas Anderson has always sensed something was wrong with his world. When he discovers humanity is trapped in a vast computer simulation, he must become more than human to set them free.

If you love reality-bending action, profound philosophical questions, and heroes discovering their true potential, this book is perfect for you.

Get it now."

The ***Machine Gun Method*** uses a rapid-fire combination of setting, emotion, and character: [Setting] + [Verb/Emotion] + [Character] + [Description] [Second Character] + [Description] + [Stakes] [Three Questions]

For *The Matrix*: "A simulated world. Controlled. A hacker discovering everything he knows is a lie. A mysterious rebellion. Fighting impossible odds. With humanity's freedom hanging in the balance. Can he accept the unbearable truth? Will he become something more than human? Is he truly The One?"

Each method serves different types of stories better:

- The Story Core works best for character-focused narratives
- The Three-Hook Structure excels for high-concept or genre fiction
- The Machine Gun Method shines with action-packed or thriller-style stories

Consider writing your blurb using all three methods and seeing which resonates most strongly with your story. ***Sometimes, you might even combine elements from different approaches.*** For instance, you might use the Machine Gun Method's setting introduction, followed by the Story Core's character focus, and end with the Three-Hook Structure's target audience statement.

Remember the core principles that apply ***regardless*** of method:

- Keep it between 100-250 words
- Focus on emotional connection over plot summary
- Leave questions unanswered to create intrigue
- Speak directly to your target audience

The best way to master blurb writing is to practice all three methods. Try rewriting your favorite books' blurbs using each approach. This exercise helps you understand how different structures can highlight different aspects of the same story.

HOW TO POSITION RETAILER SALES TO DRIVE DIRECT ENGAGEMENT

Many authors assume that once a reader buys a book on a retailer, the transaction is over. But in reality, that sale is just the beginning of the engagement funnel. Every retailer buyer is a potential long-term fan, but only if the author has a structured way to keep them engaged.

1. USING BOOK BACKMATTER AS A CONVERSION TOOL

A reader who finishes a book is already engaged and that's the best time to guide them toward taking the next step.

Instead of just listing other books, backmatter should include:

- **A direct call-to-action to sign up for an email list** ("Get a free bonus chapter here!").
- **A special offer that leads them to a direct sale** ("Get the exclusive hardcover edition only on my website!").
- **A preview of the next book in the series**, with a link to buy immediately.

2. OFFERING EXCLUSIVE DIRECT SALES BUNDLES FOR RETAILER READERS

Authors can increase direct sales by creating special editions, bundles, or signed copies that aren't available on retailers. For example:

- A retailer reader buys a $4.99 ebook.
- In the backmatter, they see an offer for **an exclusive signed hardcover bundle** that includes bonus material.
- They click the link, land on the author's direct store, and make a **higher-value purchase**.

This moves the reader from a casual retailer buyer to a direct-sale customer, where the author keeps 100% of the profit.

THE FULL RETAILER-TO-SUPERFAN PIPELINE

Retailer sales are only the first step in an author's ecosystem, but what happens next determines whether a reader becomes a one-time buyer or a lifelong supporter. The best authors don't just sell books on Amazon; they build systems that move readers through a structured journey, turning casual buyers into repeat customers, subscribers, and superfans.

Most authors focus all their energy on getting the sale—running promotions, optimizing retailer listings, and pushing ads to drive purchases. But the difference between an author who struggles with momentum and one who thrives long-term isn't just about acquiring readers, it's about what happens after the sale. The authors who build sustainable, six-figure careers don't just sell books; they guide readers through a journey that turns them from casual buyers into lifelong superfans.

The transition from reader to superfan doesn't happen by accident. It's a deliberate process and it starts the moment a reader finishes a book. That's the peak moment of engagement. The reader is emotionally connected to the story, the characters, and the world the author has created. This is the perfect time to capture their interest and lead them toward deeper engagement.

STEP 1: CAPTURING RETAILER BUYERS WITH AN IRRESISTIBLE NEXT STEP

Too many authors waste the backmatter of their books, assuming that readers will seek them out if they're interested. But without a clear next step, most readers simply move on to another book, often by a different author. The most successful authors design their backmatter strategically, ensuring that every retailer sale has the potential to bring the reader deeper into their ecosystem.

An effective call-to-action at the end of a book should do three things:

1. **Offer an exclusive bonus** that provides immediate value—such as a free short story, an extended epilogue, or early access to the next book in the series.
2. **Make it easy to take action** by directing the reader to a simple, memorable URL—rather than a homepage where they might get lost.
3. **Create urgency** by making the offer feel time-sensitive—giving them a reason to act **now** rather than later.

For example, instead of ending a book with:
"Thanks for reading! Check out my other books!"

A strong call-to-action would say:
"Want more of this world? Get an exclusive bonus scene and be the first to hear about my next release! → Click here now!"

By removing friction and making the next step irresistible, authors create a seamless transition from retailer sales to direct engagement, capturing readers before they drift away.

STEP 2: USING EMAIL SEQUENCES TO DEEPEN THE READER RELATIONSHIP

Getting a reader onto an email list is only the beginning. If all they receive is a generic newsletter once a month, they'll likely forget why they signed up in the first place. The true power of email marketing isn't just in selling more books, it's in building a long-term relationship that makes the reader feel personally connected to the author.

A well-crafted welcome sequence ensures that new subscribers don't just sit on an email list—they become engaged fans who are excited for the next book, Kickstarter campaign, or special edition release.

An effective welcome sequence should:

1. **Thank the reader immediately** for signing up and deliver the exclusive bonus they were promised.
2. **Introduce them to the author's world**, whether that's through behind-the-scenes content, a personal message, or insights into the next book.
3. **Guide them toward the next step**, whether that's a direct store offer, a subscription membership, or a pre-order for an upcoming release.

The goal isn't just to sell another book right away. It's to deepen the connection so the reader feels invested in the author's career. When readers feel like they're part of something bigger, they become repeat buyers, Kickstarter backers, and superfans who support every new project.

It's not just about delivering a free book and pointing to the next offer. It's about helping readers break through the blocks that stand between casual interest and lifelong fandom.

When someone signs up for your list, they're saying, *"I'm curious."* But curiosity isn't enough. They might be wondering: *Is this author for me? Will I like their style? Can I trust them to deliver stories I care about?* An effective welcome sequence addresses those doubts, not by pushing more products, but by guiding readers through what they need to know in order to fall in love with your world.

You're not just thanking them. You're showing them why your books matter. Maybe that's telling them where the story idea came from, or why certain characters exist, or giving them a behind-the-scenes look at the themes you explore. You're making them feel like they've discovered something special.

From there, it's not about rushing them into a store offer or throwing a pre-order link in their face. It's about giving them a reason to care. Once they feel invested, they'll want to know what else you're doing. And then, when the timing is right, you can show them the next step: maybe that's joining your membership, maybe it's pre-ordering your next book, or maybe it's simply staying tuned for what's coming next.

The real goal isn't to push for another sale right away. It's to create a connection so strong that the reader feels like they're part of something bigger. When that happens, they don't just buy a book. They back your Kickstarters. They subscribe. They tell their friends. They become the kind of readers who support you for years, not just for one launch.

Authors who understand this don't just build email lists—they build ecosystems. And every reader who enters that system becomes part of a long-term story that grows with every book you write.

Authors who execute this process well don't just make a sale. They build a lifelong relationship with every reader who enters their ecosystem.

HOW TO TRACK READER MOVEMENT ACROSS PLATFORMS

One of the biggest advantages of a retailer-to-superfan pipeline is that it allows authors to track and measure reader engagement, ensuring that no reader slips through the cracks.

To do this effectively, authors should:

- Use UTM tracking links in backmatter; CTAs to see how many readers click through to direct sales. A UTM (Urchin Tracking Module) is a simple bit of text you add to the end of a URL that helps you track where your traffic is coming from.
- Segment email subscribers based on entry points (Amazon buyers, direct store customers, Kickstarter backers).
- Analyze readthrough rates and engagement metrics to determine which readers are most likely to convert into superfans.

By tracking how readers move through the funnel, authors can refine their strategy over time, making sure retailer sales continue feeding into the broader ecosystem.

Many authors fall into the trap of chasing raw sales numbers, believing that more retailer purchases automatically equal more success. They focus on climbing Amazon rankings, hitting bestseller lists, or driving as many paid downloads as possible. But in reality, not all readers are created equal. A one-time Amazon buyer who reads a single book and moves on is far less valuable than a reader who becomes deeply engaged in the author's ecosystem.

A direct store customer, for example, isn't just another sale. They are a high-value reader who is far more likely to purchase multiple books over time, increasing their lifetime value, join a subscription, providing ongoing recurring revenue rather than a one-time purchase and support crowdfunding campaigns, helping fund future projects before they even launch.

Instead of focusing solely on retailer rankings or short-term ad spend, the most successful direct-selling authors prioritize long-term reader value. They understand that a reader who buys once and disappears is not as valuable as a reader who stays engaged, supports every launch, and actively spreads the word.

By shifting focus from transactional book sales to building a true reader community, authors create a business that is both more profitable and more sustainable. Rankings and raw sales numbers may look impressive, but it's reader retention, engagement, and lifetime value that ultimately define a thriving, long-term author career.

HOW TO OPTIMIZE THE RETAILER-TO-SUPERFAN PIPELINE FOR LONG-TERM SUCCESS

To make sure this pipeline runs efficiently and grows over time, authors should follow these key principles:

1. CREATE A COMPELLING "READER JOURNEY"

Every retailer buyer should have a clear, logical path toward deeper engagement.

For example:

- Amazon Buyer → Email List Opt-In → Welcome Sequence → Direct Sales Offer → Subscription Upsell

Each step should feel seamless and natural, so readers are guided into the ecosystem without feeling like they're being "sold" to.

2. AUTOMATE AS MUCH AS POSSIBLE

Manually managing reader engagement isn't scalable—but automation makes it effortless.

- Set up automated email sequences to welcome retailer readers and guide them toward deeper engagement.
- Use pre-scheduled content drops (bonus chapters, behind-the-scenes material) to keep readers engaged without constant effort.
- Create evergreen promotions that continue bringing in new readers over time.

3. CONTINUOUSLY OPTIMIZE & IMPROVE

A retailer funnel isn't static. It should be tested and refined based on real data.

- Monitor conversion rates from retailer sales to email sign-ups.
- A/B test different backmatter CTAs to see which offers drive the most engagement.
- Track how retailer readers behave over time to improve retention strategies.

The goal is to make every retailer buyer as valuable as possible, ensuring that no potential superfan is wasted.

Selling books on retailers is just the beginning. The most successful authors don't just aim for one-time purchases. They design a system that turns casual readers into lifelong superfans. Instead of relying on retailer algorithms to drive repeat sales, they take control of the reader journey, ensuring that every sale is a stepping stone toward deeper engagement.

A well-structured reader pipeline allows authors to capture and retain more readers, increasing long-term revenue per customer while reducing dependence on unpredictable marketplace changes. A reader who buys a book on Amazon or Kobo isn't just another statistic—they're a potential long-term supporter, if given the right path to follow. By creating an optimized process that leads readers from their first purchase to direct sales, subscriptions, and crowdfunding support, authors build a business that isn't at the mercy of retailer algorithms.

Retailers provide incredible reach, but what happens after the sale is what determines an author's long-term success. Without a clear system in place, readers who love a book might never engage again. But with the right strategy, an author can guide them toward email sign-ups, direct store purchases, and subscription memberships, ensuring they remain connected for future releases.

For authors looking to future-proof their careers, designing a retailer-to-superfan pipeline isn't optional. The authors who master this process don't just sell books; they create a thriving, sustainable business that grows stronger with every new release.

KICKSTARTER

For many authors, the traditional path to self-publishing feels linear. You write the book, put it up for sale on Amazon, market it with ads, and hope for the best. Kickstarter disrupts that model entirely. Instead of throwing a book into the marketplace and waiting for readers to find it, authors can use crowdfunding to test demand, engage an audience before launch, and generate revenue upfront.

Still, despite its potential, many authors hesitate to embrace Kickstarter. Some see it as a tool only for established names, others believe it's too much work, and many assume that success on Kickstarter is separate from success in long-term publishing. The reality is different. Kickstarter isn't just a way to fund a book. It's a launch strategy that fuels everything that comes after it.

The authors who succeed on Kickstarter don't treat it as a one-time event. They understand that a crowdfunding campaign isn't just about raising money. It's about building a foundation for lifelong reader engagement, direct sales, and a self-sustaining publishing career. Moreso, Kickstarter is a renewable resource, just like a retailer, and there are readers who *only* buy on Kickstarter.

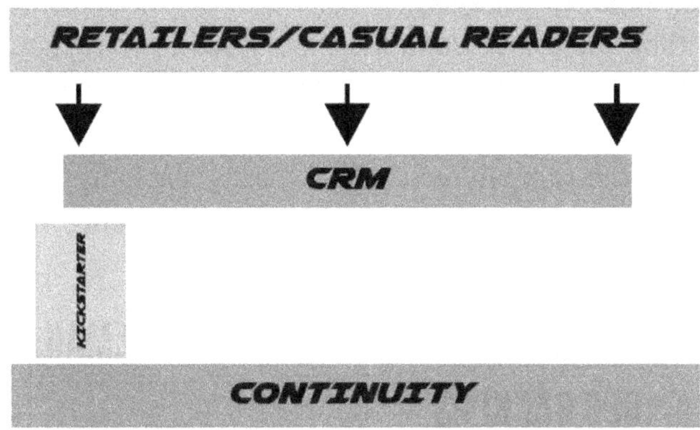

WHY KICKSTARTER GENERATES THE HIGHEST REVENUE PER READER

Most authors focus on selling books for a set price often defaulting to $4.99 for an ebook and $14.99 for a paperback, maybe charging a little more for a hardcover. They aim for volume, pushing sales through Amazon, Kobo, or direct stores, hoping to make up for narrow profit margins with sheer numbers.

Kickstarter flips that model. Instead of selling books at a fixed price, it invites readers to support a project at different levels, often paying significantly more than they would on a traditional retailer. A reader who might only spend $4.99 on an ebook elsewhere might pledge $25 on Kickstarter for a signed edition with bonus content, or even $100 for a collector's box set. The financial difference is staggering with Kickstarter backers often willing to spend 5-10x more per book than the average retailer customer.

Backers aren't just paying for a book. They're investing in the author, the project, and the experience of being part of something from the ground up. This emotional connection makes them more likely to continue supporting the author long after the campaign ends, whether by backing future projects, subscribing to memberships, or becoming high-value direct store customers.

HOW KICKSTARTER BUILDS A HIGH-VALUE EMAIL LIST OF ENGAGED BACKERS

The biggest challenge for many authors is finding their audience. On Amazon, an author is competing with thousands of other books, hoping the right readers stumble across their work. With Facebook ads, they're paying to get in front of potential buyers, often at a high cost. Kickstarter, on the other hand, allows authors to build an audience that is deeply invested from day one.

Every backer on Kickstarter provided their direct contact information, meaning they can be directly contacted long after the campaign is over (*please give them the option to opt-in, though*). Unlike retailer sales, where authors have no idea who their buyers are, Kickstarter provides a direct line of communication with every reader who supported the launch.

This is invaluable. A well-run Kickstarter can generate hundreds or even thousands of highly engaged subscribers, forming the foundation for future book launches, direct sales, and subscription memberships. Instead of chasing readers through paid advertising, authors who launch on Kickstarter start their careers with an existing, engaged audience.

THE DIFFERENCE BETWEEN KICKSTARTER AND A TRADITIONAL BOOK LAUNCH

A typical book launch is reactive. Authors publish their book and wait to see how it performs. They might push for pre-orders, run some ads, or try to generate early reviews, but the process is largely the same as every other book on the market. Kickstarter, on the other hand, flips the script entirely.

Instead of launching a book and hoping for sales, authors can use Kickstarter to validate demand before the book is even published. They gauge interest, test pricing, and engage their audience before the book goes to print. The campaign itself becomes a marketing engine, creating buzz and excitement long before the book is officially available.

This approach has a cascading effect. A successful Kickstarter creates momentum that carries into retailer launches, direct sales, and future crowdfunding campaigns. The energy generated during the campaign doesn't just fade away. It builds anticipation for everything that comes next.

Just look at Brandon Sanderson. The books that he raised $41 million to release were sold to publishers and became huge sellers on retailers because everyone was talking about them. It's been true in my career as well. The books that bump on Kickstarter also bump on retailers.

Many authors see Kickstarter as something to try after they've built an audience elsewhere. They assume they need a large platform before attempting crowdfunding. But the truth is, Kickstarter is one of the best tools for authors who are just starting out, but maybe not in the way you think.

While the platform itself provides built-in discoverability, allowing authors to tap into Kickstarter's existing community of readers looking for new books, newer authors can also use it to experiment and refine their strategy in a low-risk environment. Because backers pledge money before the book is produced, authors can adjust their plans based on real-world data, rather than guessing what readers might want.

It's the ability to use Kickstarter as a testing ground that is the main reason we tell people to use it as the first step in their publishing journey.

HOW TO STRUCTURE A KICKSTARTER FOR MAXIMUM LONG-TERM IMPACT

A Kickstarter campaign is more than just a way to fund a book. It's the start of an author's relationship with their readers. Every backer who pledges isn't just pre-ordering a book; they're buying into the author's vision, supporting the creative process, and becoming part of something bigger. When structured correctly, a Kickstarter campaign doesn't just fund a single book. Done well, it helps lay the foundation for an author's entire career.

But not all campaigns are created equal. Many authors launch their first Kickstarter with little thought beyond covering production costs, failing to recognize the potential for long-term engagement. A well-structured campaign isn't just about hitting a funding goal; it's about guiding backers into a journey that continues long after the campaign ends.

A common mistake authors make is treating a Kickstarter campaign like a **one-time event**, as if it exists in isolation from the rest of their publishing plans. They think in terms of short-term goals: "I just need to hit my funding target." But a well-structured campaign does more than fund a book, it funnels readers into an ecosystem where they continue engaging, buying, and supporting the author long-term.

At its core, a Kickstarter campaign should:

- Introduce new readers to the author's work in a compelling way.
- Encourage deeper engagement through carefully designed rewards and stretch goals.
- Guide backers into direct sales and subscription models after the campaign ends.

This means every part of the campaign—from the rewards to the updates to the fulfillment strategy—should be designed to carry momentum forward rather than letting it die once the campaign is over.

HOW TO DESIGN REWARD TIERS THAT LEAD TO LONG-TERM ENGAGEMENT

Kickstarter campaigns can be powerful vehicles for funding your book, building buzz, and forging deeper connections with your readers. One of the most important decisions you'll make when setting up a campaign is deciding how many reward tiers to offer and what each tier should include. There are two main schools of thought on this:

1. **Keep it Simple:** Offer a few tiers like a digital copy, a paperback, and maybe a signed edition to limit complexity.
2. **Aim for Engagement:** Offer multiple tiers with exclusive items, premium editions, and experiences that keep readers connected over the long term.

Both approaches can work, but they serve different purposes and come with different risks.

THE "SIMPLE" CAMPAIGN

This approach keeps reward tiers to a minimum. For a book project, which might mean:

- A digital edition at a low pledge level.
- A paperback edition at a mid-range pledge level.
- A signed or limited-edition hardcover for fans who want something special.

WHY KEEP IT SIMPLE?

- **Lower Risk and Complexity:** Fewer reward tiers mean less logistical juggling during fulfillment. You won't need to worry about ordering specialized merchandise or orchestrating multiple shipments.
- **Great for First Timers:** If you're new to Kickstarter, or if your audience is completely unfamiliar with crowdfunding, simplicity can be a good way to test the waters.
- **Validates Demand:** You find out whether people want to buy directly from you without overcommitting to a complex production or distribution plan.

DRAWBACKS OF SIMPLICITY

- **Potentially Lower Per-Backer Spend:** Without more elaborate or exclusive tiers, you might see smaller average pledges. People who would pay extra for special editions or bundled merchandise won't have the option.
- **Less "Buzz":** Some argue that big, exciting rewards generate more attention. If you only have simple tiers, you might miss out on headlines like "Author Offers Ultra-Exclusive, Hand-Bound Leather Edition."

THE "EXPERIENCE" CAMPAIGN

This philosophy suggests offering multiple, tiered experiences or collectibles that go beyond just a single book. Examples might include:

- **Early Access to Future Books:** A digital bundle that guarantees you'll receive the next novel before its official release date.
- **Exclusive Hardcovers and Collectibles:** A special edition with custom artwork, personal notes, or signatures that make the book feel more like an event than a product.
- **Ongoing Community Access:** Membership in a private reader group, a dedicated Slack or Discord channel, or behind-the-scenes updates that keep readers engaged well after the campaign ends.
- **High-Tier Pledges with Direct Sales Bundles:** Perhaps a year-long subscription to future works, or a box set that includes multiple titles plus merchandise.

WHY OFFER A BIGGER EXPERIENCE?

- **Higher Funding Per Backer:** By appealing to your most devoted fans, you can substantially increase your average pledge.
- **Long-Term Engagement:** When readers feel they're part of something exclusive, they're more likely to stick around for future books or campaigns.
- **Direct Sales Momentum:** If you're planning to sell future titles directly, offering add-ons and exclusive bundles now can begin training your audience to buy from you instead of just relying on retail channels.

DRAWBACKS TO COMPLEXITY

- **Greater Stress & Fulfillment Overhead:** Handling special editions, shipping multiple items, or providing ongoing community events can be time-consuming and complicated—especially if you don't have a team.
- **Uncertain Audience Appetite:** If you're not sure how big or enthusiastic your audience is, you could end up with a lot of unsold or unclaimed rewards.

FINDING THE RIGHT BALANCE

For many authors, especially if it's their first or second time on Kickstarter, there's a middle ground between "one digital file" and "twenty tiers of collectibles."

Consider these strategies:

1. **Start Small, But Add One Premium Option**

   - Include your basic tiers (e.g., digital, paperback, signed hardcover).

- Offer a single "special" tier for fans who want more: a personalized letter, limited-run cover art, or a short Zoom meet-and-greet.
- This way, you learn if higher-end rewards resonate with your audience without juggling a dozen complex fulfillment tasks.

2. **Use Stretch Goals to Unlock Extras**

- Begin with simple tiers, then announce new rewards or editions as you pass certain funding milestones.
- This approach keeps initial complexity low. If the campaign overperforms, you can introduce extras like a slipcase edition, an exclusive bookmark, or a behind-the-scenes eBook.

3. **Test an "Anniversary" book**

- If you already have a title that's proven popular, use it as your Kickstarter offering. People know they like it; you know what to expect in terms of demand.
- Add a new cover, a bonus chapter, or an author's note to create a collectible feel.
- If the campaign succeeds, you can build from there with future Kickstarters.

4. **Bring Back a "Second Chance" book**

- Similar to the above, choose a book that's a fan favorite but didn't get the launch it deserved, and give it the star treatment
- Add a new cover, a bonus chapter, or an author's note to create a collectible feel.

- If the campaign succeeds, you can turn that failure into a bestseller.

5. **Offer a Taste of Community, But Don't Over-Promise**

   - A small private Facebook or Discord group might be enough to gauge interest in a community tier.
   - If backers love it, you can offer more extensive community rewards in later projects.
   - If you feel overwhelmed by moderation or extra work, you can downsize or close it gracefully after the campaign.

WHY SIMPLICITY CAN BE A SMART FIRST MOVE

Some Kickstarter experts focus heavily on maximizing the "experience" aspect right from the start. While it's true that higher-end, exclusive tiers can lead to larger pledges, it can also be a lot for a first-time creator to handle.

Remember: The main goal is to ensure your campaign is a success, both for you and for your readers. If complex tiers result in confusion or burnout, that can damage trust and make it harder to run campaigns in the future.

By starting with something you already know your audience loves, like an anniversary edition of a fan-favorite novel or a special reissue of a "second chance" book, you can confirm the basics: Do your readers enjoy supporting you directly? Are they willing to pay a premium for extras? Would they be interested in a community or future bundles?

The answers to these questions will guide your next move. If there's enthusiastic uptake and people clamor for more, you can plan bigger campaigns with confidence. If you find that simple tiers work but nothing beyond that sells, you'll know to keep future projects streamlined.

WHY STRETCH GOALS AND COMMUNITY ENGAGEMENT MATTER

Many authors see stretch goals as an afterthought, something to add if the campaign does well. But the best Kickstarter campaigns plan stretch goals in advance, not just to increase funding but to keep backers engaged and excited throughout the campaign.

A good stretch goal strategy:

- **Encourages existing backers to upgrade their pledges** to unlock exclusive perks.
- **Creates excitement and urgency**, keeping backers engaged throughout the campaign instead of just pledging once and forgetting about it.
- **Adds value for backers without increasing the author's workload.**
- **Gives you more reasons to reach out to your backers**.

Instead of thinking of stretch goals as **extra work**, authors should design them to **build reader loyalty**. For example, successful authors have used stretch goals to:

- **Unlock bonus stories or side content** that later becomes part of a subscription model.

- **Add backer-exclusive content**, creating **a strong incentive for readers to continue supporting future campaigns**.
- **Tie into direct sales strategies**, like unlocking a new special edition that will later be available on the author's webstore.

The best stretch goals aren't just about sweetening the deal for your current backers. They also lay the groundwork for ongoing engagement long after your campaign ends. Think of stretch goals as a bridge between the excitement of the Kickstarter and the long-term relationship you want to foster with your readers. Adding future-focused elements—like early access to upcoming releases, invitations to exclusive online events, or limited-edition collectibles—turns stretch goals into opportunities for deeper, sustained connection.

Personally, I prefer unveiling new rewards or bonuses on a weekly schedule (or even daily perks to delight readers) rather than tying them strictly to funding milestones. This approach gives me greater control over my outreach, allowing me to plan exactly when to re-engage backers instead of waiting passively for the campaign to cross a particular threshold.

Each week's "unlock" becomes a natural reason to email, post updates, and drum up fresh excitement. It also provides a steady stream of talking points for social media, encouraging backers to spread the word and enticing newcomers to join in before the next reveal. By pacing your stretch goal announcements, you transform your campaign into an ongoing event keeping backers curious, engaged, and eager to see what you'll offer next

TESTING ON KICKSTARTER

Most authors launch their books with no real data about how their readers prefer to buy. They price their books based on market averages, package their editions based on what's common, and hope that readers will respond well. But hope isn't a strategy, and launching without testing is a recipe for lost revenue and missed opportunities.

Kickstarter eliminates this uncertainty. Instead of blindly setting a price on Amazon or designing a direct sales offer based on guesswork, authors can use Kickstarter as a real-world testing ground. The platform provides hard data on what readers are willing to pay, what formats they prefer, and what upgrades they're most excited about, all before the book ever reaches retail or direct sales.

Traditional publishers spend months conducting market research before releasing a book. They test covers, experiment with pricing, and gauge audience demand long before a book ever reaches shelves. Every decision, from packaging to distribution strategy, is backed by data. In contrast, many indie authors skip this step entirely, going straight to launch without any real validation. They finalize covers, set prices, and choose formats based on intuition rather than actual reader demand.

Kickstarter offers indie authors a built-in market testing system that eliminates the guesswork. Instead of launching blindly and hoping a book will sell, authors can use a crowdfunding campaign to gather real-world data before committing to production decisions. The platform allows authors to experiment with different pricing structures, test packaging options, and gauge interest in special editions, all while funding the book in advance.

Through Kickstarter, authors can see exactly which price tiers perform best, giving them insight into how much readers are truly willing to pay for different formats. They can test demand for paperbacks versus hardcovers, standard editions versus collector's editions, and determine which options are worth producing at scale. Add-ons, stretch goals, and exclusive content provide another layer of insight—revealing what readers value most and what they are willing to pay extra for.

This kind of real-time market research is invaluable. Instead of guessing what will sell, authors can let their audience decide, ensuring that every future launch is optimized for maximum revenue and engagement. Used like this Kickstarter isn't just a funding platform. it's a powerful tool for shaping the most profitable and reader-driven version of a book launch.

TESTING PRICING: HOW KICKSTARTER REVEALS WHAT READERS WILL ACTUALLY PAY

One of the biggest challenges authors face is knowing how to price their books. Charge too much, and readers won't buy. Charge too little, and the author leaves money on the table.

Kickstarter solves this problem by allowing authors to test multiple price points in real time. By setting up different reward tiers, authors can see exactly what readers are willing to pay, not just for the book itself, but for exclusive editions, signed copies, and premium add-ons.

For example, an author might structure their tiers like this:

- **$10** – Digital Edition
- **$25** – Paperback Edition
- **$50** – Signed Hardcover + Bonus Content
- **$100** – Collector's Box Set + Exclusive Art Print

If the $50 tier far outsells the $25 tier, that's a clear signal that readers are willing to pay more for premium experiences.

TESTING PACKAGING: HOW TO FIND OUT WHAT READERS WANT BEFORE YOU PRINT

Every author wrestles with decisions about which formats to offer. Should they invest in hardcover editions? Do readers even want signed books? Will special packaging options actually sell?

Instead of making these decisions blindly, Kickstarter allows authors to offer multiple formats and see which ones backers prefer. If a limited edition hardcover gets strong support, it makes sense to offer that format in future direct sales. If a particular reward tier struggles, it might not be worth producing in bulk.

What Packaging Variables Can Be Tested on Kickstarter?

- **Paperback vs. Hardcover Demand** – Are readers willing to pay more for a premium edition?
- **Special Editions vs. Standard Releases** – Is there demand for collector's versions?
- **Signed vs. Unsigned Copies** – Are readers paying extra for personalized books?
- **Exclusive Add-Ons** – Do readers want bookmarks, slipcases, or art prints?

TESTING ADD-ONS AND STRETCH GOALS: WHAT EXTRAS ARE READERS WILLING TO PAY FOR?

Many authors assume that books are the only thing readers care about, but Kickstarter often proves otherwise. Readers frequently want more than just the book. They're interested in behind-the-scenes content, exclusive merchandise, and unique collector's items.

Or at least they say they do. Kickstarter allows authors to test which extras resonate most before investing in large production runs. Instead of guessing what readers want, authors can see real purchasing behavior in action.

Some of the most popular extras include:

- Exclusive bonus stories or novellas.
- Limited-run artwork or illustrated editions.
- Merchandise like mugs, T-shirts, or enamel pins.
- Behind-the-scenes access (author Q&As, live chats, digital perks).

By testing these extras as stretch goals or add-ons, authors can identify the most profitable options before scaling them in direct sales.

HOW TO COLLECT READER DATA FROM KICKSTARTER FOR FUTURE LAUNCHES

Kickstarter isn't just a funding tool; it's also a data goldmine. Every pledge provides valuable insights into reader behavior, which can be used to refine future book launches. How do you collect data?

1. **Backer Surveys** – Ask readers why they backed, what formats they prefer, and what they'd like to see next.
2. **Pledge Patterns** – Analyze which tiers performed best and adjust pricing accordingly.
3. **Repeat Backer Behavior** – Track how many backers support multiple campaigns to measure retention.

Authors who pay attention to Kickstarter analytics and backer feedback can refine not just future crowdfunding campaigns, but also their entire publishing business.

KICKSTARTER AS A HIGH-VALUE MARKETING ASSET

Many authors think of Kickstarter purely as a way to raise funds for a single project, but the real benefit goes well beyond one campaign. Each Kickstarter you run can be used to create evergreen marketing assets that help propel your career for years to come. Yes, building a campaign can be time-consuming and sometimes expensive, but that's because building marketing assets is exhausting. If you do it right, you can build these assets now and use them in the following pieces of the stack, which is another reason why Kickstarter comes first.

When you invest in crafting compelling rewards, writing polished sales copy, building emails and creative content, and networking with potential backers, you're not just funding a book—you're laying the groundwork for all your future marketing. From the Kickstarter page itself to the behind-the-scenes videos, bonus content, and stretch-goal ideas, these materials form a library of assets that can be reused and adapted for:

- **Future Book Launches:** The same polished copy or exclusive materials can migrate to your direct-sales website or be recycled as special-edition bundles later.
- **Email Marketing and Automations:** The email sequences you create to nurture backers can be tweaked for new subscribers who discover you after the campaign.
- **Social Media & Ads:** The teaser images and videos you made for the Kickstarter become ready-made content for Facebook, Instagram, TikTok, or anywhere you run ads.

Running a Kickstarter campaign demands more front-loaded work like planning rewards, crafting a compelling page, filming videos, and managing backer communication. There may also be added costs for things like professional design, promotional materials, or higher-quality reward items, but this upfront investment is work you will eventually have to do anyway. So, you might as well get paid to do it from your campaign.

HOW KICKSTARTER MOMENTUM BOOSTS RETAILER & DIRECT SALES SUCCESS

A successful Kickstarter isn't just about funding a book. It's about fueling everything that comes next. Many authors see Kickstarter as a one-time event, a way to get their book into the world before moving on to retailer sales and direct sales. But the truth is, Kickstarter momentum doesn't stop when the campaign ends.

A well-executed Kickstarter creates a spillover effect, one that amplifies sales across Amazon, Kobo, Barnes and

Noble, Google Play, and Apple Books, increases direct store revenue, and supercharges future crowdfunding campaigns. The key to long-term success is understanding how to harness that momentum, ensuring that the energy of a Kickstarter launch carries forward into every part of an author's business.

When a Kickstarter campaign performs well, it doesn't just fund the book. It creates a surge of reader excitement. Backers talk about the project. They share updates. They generate buzz before the book is even available to the general public. This pre-release excitement has a direct and measurable impact on retailer sales, so make sure to have a pre-order for the book up before the book goes live on Kickstarter. People will go buy the book on retailers if your book is available there, since not everyone wants to buy on Kickstarter. Just set your date 90 days after the campaign ends, or more, so the backers get it early.

Combined with this excitement, you should have excess revenue from the campaign you can dump into ads to help amplify your launch even more, creating an even bigger launch.

For many authors who adopt a Kickstarter-first strategy, the difference is night and day. Instead of launching on Amazon with zero momentum, they hit the marketplace with an army of enthusiastic readers already in place who have been anticipating the book for months, who are eager to leave reviews, and who are primed to spread the word. This early surge doesn't just improve first-week sales; it has long-term benefits, ensuring that the book remains visible in rankings and retailer recommendations long after the initial launch period.

Kickstarter isn't just a way to fund a book. It's a launch strategy that makes every other part of the publishing process stronger. By the time the book reaches wide distribution, it already has traction, putting it miles ahead of a typical cold launch.

BUILDING A KICKSTARTER-TO-DIRECT SALES PIPELINE FOR FUTURE CAMPAIGNS

For many authors, a Kickstarter campaign feels like a single event—something to plan, execute, and then move on from. They launch, they fulfill, and then they start thinking about what's next. But for the most successful authors, Kickstarter isn't just a one-time fundraising tool—it's a recurring, scalable system that feeds into direct sales, subscriptions, and future campaigns.

A single Kickstarter campaign can be life-changing, but a repeatable Kickstarter strategy can transform an author's entire business model. Instead of constantly chasing new readers on Amazon or pouring money into Facebook ads, authors who build a Kickstarter-to-direct sales pipeline create a sustainable cycle where each campaign builds upon the last, making the next launch easier, bigger, and more profitable.

Kickstarter campaigns create highly engaged backers, but many authors make the mistake of losing connection with them after fulfillment. Once the book is shipped, there's often no structured follow-up, leaving backers to drift away until the next campaign, if they remember to return at all.

The goal of a Kickstarter-to-direct sales pipeline is to ensure that backers don't just support one book, but become lifelong customers. This means moving them into a system where they continue buying books, subscribing to memberships, and engaging with the author's world.

1. CREATE AN IMMEDIATE POST-CAMPAIGN OFFER

The best time to transition a Kickstarter backer into a direct sales customer is right after they've pledged, while they're still engaged, excited, and in a buying mindset.

Instead of waiting months for fulfillment to reconnect, successful authors:

- Offer **a limited-time special edition or signed bundle** only available in their direct store.
- Give backers a **discount code for future purchases**, incentivizing them to visit the author's website.
- Introduce them to **a membership or subscription program** that provides ongoing access to exclusive content.

Backers are already willing to spend more than the average retailer buyer, giving them an easy next step ensures they continue supporting the author.

2. KEEP BACKERS ENGAGED BETWEEN CAMPAIGNS

A major mistake authors make is going silent between Kickstarter launches, treating their backers like temporary customers instead of a permanent audience.

Instead of disappearing, successful authors:

- **Send regular updates**—behind-the-scenes content, early previews, or personal insights into the writing process.
- **Involve backers in decision-making**, such as cover selection or special edition perks.
- **Provide exclusive digital bonuses**, keeping backers engaged even if they aren't making a purchase right away.

The goal isn't just to keep selling, it's to make backers feel like they are part of the journey, ensuring they are excited for the next campaign before it even launches.

A single Kickstarter campaign can be powerful, but a Kickstarter-first business model turns crowdfunding into a repeatable launch strategy. Instead of releasing books directly to retailers or relying on unpredictable ad-driven sales, authors can use Kickstarter as their primary launch platform, ensuring every book is funded before it's even produced.

Authors who run **multiple Kickstarter campaigns** see an exponential effect:

1. **Repeat backers increase with each campaign**, as existing supporters return for future books.
2. **Funding amounts grow over time**, as authors refine their offers and build credibility.
3. **Future launches become easier**, as readers expect and anticipate each new campaign.

Instead of starting from scratch every time, authors with a recurring Kickstarter strategy build momentum, making each campaign bigger and more successful than the last.

CREATING A SUSTAINABLE KICKSTARTER SYSTEM

For a Kickstarter-first strategy to work long-term, it can't rely on constant manual effort. Running a campaign requires energy, but the real challenge isn't just funding one book. It's structuring a system that keeps backers engaged between campaigns while allowing the author to focus on writing and growing their business. Without a clear, automated follow-up process, many authors find themselves exhausted after a successful campaign, struggling to maintain momentum before their next launch.

Kickstarter isn't just a funding tool. It's a powerful publishing strategy for authors who want full control over their careers. Instead of relying on traditional retail models that require high volume and low margins, Kickstarter-first authors take ownership of their launches, their revenue, and their reader relationships.

By using Kickstarter as the first step in every book launch, authors can:

- **Fund books upfront**, eliminating financial risk and avoiding out-of-pocket production costs.
- **Build direct relationships with readers**, ensuring they aren't reliant on retailer algorithms or third-party platforms.
- **Create a scalable launch system**, where each campaign grows larger and more profitable than the last.

The difference between Kickstarter-first authors and those who rely solely on retailers is confidence. Instead of launching books into the unknown—hoping for algorithmic visibility or chasing unpredictable trends—Kickstarter-first authors launch with a guaranteed audience already waiting. They control their revenue, retain their readers, and grow a sustainable, high-revenue business that supports them for the long term.

LANDING PAGES

You've run a successful Kickstarter, you've optimized the page, and you've proven that readers will literally open their wallets for your pitch. When the campaign ends, most authors assume the magic ends with it. *It doesn't have to.*

The best way to keep that momentum going is to **take what you already know works**—the Kickstarter page—and **transplant it onto your own website**. Once it's there, you can continue selling your series indefinitely, using the exact copy that converted real people into paying backers.

Most people tell you to optimize using ads, which is important, but instead of judging success based on clicks, you could just use your already optimized page as a starting point to build your publishing empire. This is the workflow.

STEP 1: RUN (AND OPTIMIZE) YOUR KICKSTARTER

Kickstarter is your live testing ground. Every time a new backer pledges, you get immediate proof that your headline, images, and product description speak to actual buyers. Whenever something **doesn't** work—maybe nobody's biting at a certain pledge tier or a stretch goal—the data shows you. You adjust the copy, tweak the visuals, or reorganize your rewards, then watch to see if conversions improve.

Over the course of your campaign, you're performing **the ultimate A/B test**. Instead of paying for ads and crossing your fingers, you're seeing real transactions happen in real time. By the final day of the campaign, you have a **battle-tested** pitch that resonates with readers.

STEP 2: COPY IT TO YOUR WEBSITE

Once your Kickstarter concludes, the page itself becomes static. People can still visit, but no more pledges roll in. So rather than let that proven pitch die, **copy everything**—the layout, the images, and (most importantly) the messaging—onto a dedicated page on your own site. Use something like Elementor, Themify, Optimizepress, or something similar to make it look nice.

If your Kickstarter video was a strong opener, embed it on your new page. If your bullet points or reward descriptions really hit home, adapt them to describe your series, box set, or ongoing subscription.

Yes, you might make small edits—removing time-sensitive phrases like "pledge before the campaign ends!" and replacing them with "buy now." But the heart of your persuasive copy, the text that sold your readers in the first place, remains intact.

STEP 3: SELL YOUR SERIES INDEFINITELY

On Kickstarter, the excitement is tied to a countdown clock. That urgency is fantastic for generating pledges, but it also means the momentum stops once the campaign is over. Luckily, you can add things like evergreen countdown timers to replicate that urgency forever.

Think of it as flipping a switch from "limited-time campaign" to "evergreen sales funnel." Whether people hear about you three months after the Kickstarter or three years later, they'll land on a page that's already proven to convert.

STEP 4: KEEP OPTIMIZING WITH HEAT MAPS AND SESSION RECORDINGS

Once you have your new sales page live, you can track visitor behavior even more closely than you did on Kickstarter. Tools like heat maps, click tracking, and session recordings show you exactly how people move through your page:

- Where do they pause?
- Which images do they hover over?
- At what point do they stop scrolling?

These insights let you refine your pitch further. Maybe you need a bigger "Buy Now" button, or a different color scheme, or a more prominent mention of your main character's conflict. Over time, these tiny tweaks can lead to significant increases in conversion—making your page even stronger than it was on Kickstarter.

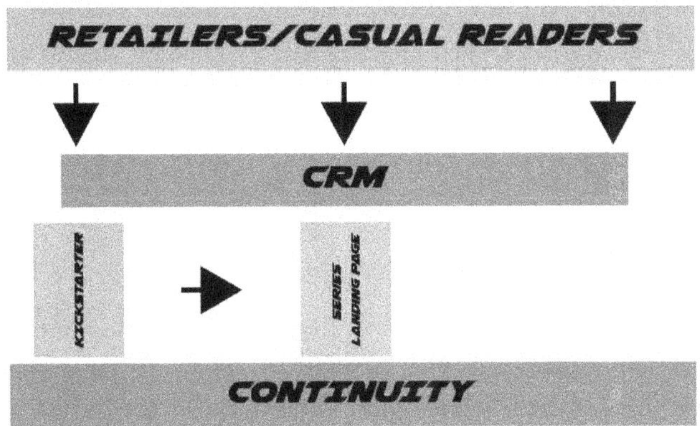

WHY NOT A FULL SHOPIFY SETUP?

Building out a complete e-commerce store can be **overkill** if you're only looking to sell a single book, a series, or a small handful of products. Maintaining multiple product listings, custom shipping rules, and a full storefront is time-consuming and often unnecessary at this stage. A simple, dedicated page with a secure checkout link (or a simple payment integration) is enough to keep the sales flowing—without burying new readers under too many choices.

WHY THIS MATTERS

Too many authors treat a Kickstarter campaign like a one-time event. They get a boost of funds and then move on, leaving behind the best piece of sales copy they ever created. By migrating your proven Kickstarter page to your own platform and continuing to optimize, you generate **ongoing sales** well beyond the campaign without getting bogged down. You're still selling one offer on one page, which means you don't need any of the fancy plugins, Shopify, or even really learning much of anything new.

In short, you're not leaving money on the table. You're turning a high-energy crowdfunding moment into a perpetual, always-on sales machine.

A successful Kickstarter campaign might give you a burst of backers, but it doesn't guarantee ongoing sales. The moment the campaign ends, sales die. **A dedicated landing page** solves this problem and gives you the customers forever(ish).

These small steps keep your audience engaged instead of letting them slip through the cracks. You're not asking them to navigate a sprawling e-commerce site or browse ten different pages. You're giving them one place to click, one place to learn more, and one place to buy.

WHAT TO USE TO BUILD YOUR PAGE

Many authors get overwhelmed by the idea of building an entire Shopify store—managing product listings, shipping settings, checkout pages, and so forth. If you're primarily focused on funneling post-Kickstarter visitors to **one** book series (or a small handful of products), a single optimized landing page is often easier and faster to maintain. You can still link out to your preferred payment processor (PayPal, Stripe, etc.) or host digital downloads behind a simple paywall—without the overhead of a full e-commerce solution.

1. Elementor (WordPress Plugin)

- **Why It's Simple:** Elementor offers a drag-and-drop interface, so you can visually build pages without coding. You can quickly rearrange elements—like headlines, images, or call-to-action buttons—by dragging them where you want.

- **Advantages:**

    o Extensive template library for quick starts.

    o Highly customizable, so you can tweak every element to match your brand.

    o Integrates easily with most email marketing services.

- **Ideal Use Case:** If you already have a WordPress site (or are comfortable setting one up) and you want full creative control over your page's design.

2. Themify (WordPress Theme + Builder)

- **Why It's Simple:** Themify is a theme framework that includes its own builder, which again uses a drag-and-drop system. It comes with pre-designed layouts specifically aimed at conversions.

- **Advantages:**

    - Built-in design elements like sliders, feature boxes, and calls-to-action.

    - Good for beginners who want a cohesive theme and page builder in one.

    - Regular updates mean you're always getting new design features.

- **Ideal Use Case:** If you prefer an "all-in-one" WordPress theme and page builder solution that meshes seamlessly, without juggling too many plugins.

3. OptimizePress (WordPress Plugin)

- **Why It's Simple:** OptimizePress focuses almost exclusively on high-conversion landing pages, sales pages, and membership portals. It's designed to help marketers and authors create funnel-like pages without needing a developer.

- **Advantages:**

    - Built-in templates optimized for sales funnels, lead captures, and product launches.

    - Easy integration with popular email marketing platforms (e.g., MailChimp, ConvertKit).

- o Step-by-step tools for setting up membership areas or gated content, if you plan to offer more than just books.

- **Ideal Use Case:** If your main concern is **conversion** and you want templates specifically designed to sell digital products (like books), webinars, or courses.

Any of these WordPress-based tools—**Elementor, Themify, OptimizePress,** or something else—can help you repurpose your successful Kickstarter copy quickly and keep selling your book or series indefinitely. You don't have to be a web developer or a design pro; just pick the plugin or theme that best matches your comfort level. By focusing on **one** high-conversion landing page instead of an entire online store, you'll save time, cut out complexity, and maintain a streamlined path for your readers to follow—well after your Kickstarter campaign has wrapped up.

THE ROLE OF TESTING IN OPTIMIZING LANDING PAGES

No landing page works perfectly right away. Many authors set up a page, assume it's effective, and never revisit it. But without real data on how readers interact with the page, there's no way to know what's working and what isn't.

This is where testing becomes essential. Tools like Hotjar, Crazy Egg, and Microsoft Clarity allow authors to see how visitors behave on the page.

- **Heat maps** show where readers are clicking, scrolling, and stopping, helping authors understand which sections grab attention and which are being ignored.

- **Session recordings** track individual reader behavior, revealing friction points that might be preventing conversions.
- **A/B testing** allows authors to experiment with different headlines, CTAs, and special offers to see which versions drive the most engagement.

For example, one author used heat maps to discover that most readers weren't scrolling far enough to see the call-to-action on their landing page. By moving the "Buy Now" button higher on the page, they increased conversion rates by 28%, generating thousands in additional sales.

Landing pages aren't static. They should evolve based on real reader behavior.

HOW TO BUILD A HIGH-CONVERTING SERIES LANDING PAGE

The best landing pages don't feel like sterile "sales" pages. They feel like a natural conversation meant to get people excited to buy your series. No matter how somebody finds your landing page, it should *guide* them to a clear, obvious next step, without requiring them to navigate an entire online store.

A series landing page is the natural next step for *anyone* who discovers your work whether they found you through a friend's recommendation, an online ad, or sheer curiosity. If you already honed a compelling Kickstarter page for your series, don't reinvent the wheel. Repurpose that same proven copy, layout, and messaging to create a permanent home for new readers. Here's the stack:

1. THE HOOK: IMMEDIATELY SHOW THEM WHAT THEY'RE GETTING

When someone arrives on your page, they should see **exactly** why your series is worth their time. If your Kickstarter headline said, "Enter a World of Myth and Magic—Start Reading Today," keep it! That single phrase attracted backers, so it'll grab new readers too.

- **Don't say:** "Welcome to my page."
- **Do say:** "Ready for an Epic Adventure? Start the Series Now."

Your headline needs to spark curiosity and highlight what's special about your series.

2. THE OFFER: CLARIFY THE VALUE OF YOUR SERIES

You already know what excited people during the Kickstarter—the premise, the unique characters, the exclusive world-building. Put that front and center. Show new readers how they can get the same amazing experience your backers enjoyed:

- **Bundle or Series Access**
  - "Get the complete series in one easy download."
- **Exclusive Edition or Perks**
  - "Receive signed digital art or behind-the-scenes notes—only here."
- **Direct Purchase Benefits**
  - "By buying here, you support the author directly—no middleman."

Your goal is to convert interest into action. If they liked the premise, let them know exactly what they'll get when they dive deeper.

3. THE CALL-TO-ACTION: MAKE IT CRYSTAL CLEAR

One page, **one** primary action. It could be:

- **"Start the Series Now"** (purchase or download)
- **"Claim Your Exclusive Story Extras"** (sign-up form)
- **"Join the Adventure"** (email capture for future releases)

Reuse the language that worked during Kickstarter's peak. That proven CTA—"Pledge" or "Get Access"—can become "Get Your Copy" or "Unlock the Series." The main thing is to keep it unambiguous and easy to find.

4. URGENCY: GIVE THEM A REASON TO ACT NOW

Yes, this is an **evergreen** page, but urgency still motivates, especially if you're using an evergreen countdown timer that actually locks the page when the timer runs out.

- **Limited Bonus Content**
    - "Free illustrated map for the first 500 readers."
- **Exclusive Discounts**
    - "Special price ends this weekend."
- **Author Interaction**
    - "Join now and get a personal thank-you from the author."

These aren't gimmicks. They're genuine perks that encourage immediate action, rather than the dreaded "I'll come back later."

5. TEST, REFINE, REPEAT

Your Kickstarter proved this copy *can* convert, but **new visitors** might behave differently than backers. Keep fine-tuning:

- **Heat Maps & Analytics:** Track where people click or bail.
- **A/B Testing:** Try different headlines or CTA colors to see if conversions rise.
- **Streamlined Tech:** No need for a complex store. A single page with a simple payment button or signup form is enough to move readers forward.

You spent weeks (or months) perfecting your Kickstarter page to hook readers. Now, you can keep that momentum alive by directing new visitors to the same proven messaging, just adapted to an evergreen environment. You don't need a giant storefront or brand-new funnel. You just need one clear, compelling page that communicates what your series is about and how they can get it.

By reusing and refining what already worked, you're not starting from scratch. You're capitalizing on tested copy, the exact words and visuals that made real people say, "I want to support this." For new readers, your series landing page becomes their first impression, one that's already been proven to drive excitement and action. That's how you turn a one-time Kickstarter success into a long-term sales engine for your series.

WHY MOST LANDING PAGES FAIL (AND HOW TO FIX IT)

A landing page isn't just a digital placeholder, it's a **conversion engine**. Its purpose is to **move readers from interest to action**, whether that means buying the next book, signing up for an email list, or joining a subscription. And like any machine, a landing page needs **fine-tuning** to function at its best.

Even with the right structure, many landing pages don't perform well. That's because most authors don't test and refine their pages based on how readers actually behave.

This leads us to Section 3: Testing and Optimizing a Landing Page for Maximum Conversions where we'll explore how to use heat maps, session recordings, and A/B testing to ensure every backer moves into long-term engagement.

TESTING AND OPTIMIZING A LANDING PAGE FOR MAXIMUM CONVERSIONS

Most authors assume that if a landing page is live, it's working. They set it up, add a few links, and expect backers to take action. But when they check the numbers, the results are disappointing. The page exists, but it isn't doing its job.

Without testing, an author is guessing about what works. Testing provides hard data on how readers interact with the page, revealing where they're engaging, where they're dropping off, and what needs to change.

A landing page can fail for many reasons, but the most common problems come down to clarity, structure, and engagement. If a visitor arrives and doesn't immediately understand what's being offered and why it matters to them, they will leave without taking action.

One of the biggest issues is visibility. If visitors don't scroll far enough to see the call-to-action (CTA), they never even get the chance to engage. A poorly placed CTA, buried too far down the page, results in missed opportunities and lost conversions. Even if a visitor is interested, if they don't immediately see where to click or what to do next, they will often move on.

Another common mistake is having a CTA that isn't clear or compelling. A weak or vague CTA—such as "Learn More" or "Sign Up"—doesn't create urgency or excitement. Readers need to understand, in a single glance, what they are getting and why they should take action now. A strong CTA, like "Claim Your Exclusive Bonus Chapter Now" or "Get 20% Off—Limited Time Only," gives them both direction and motivation.

Even with a well-placed CTA, a landing page can still fail if the offer isn't strong enough. Readers need to feel like they're getting something valuable in exchange for their time or money. If the incentive isn't compelling—if it's just a generic newsletter sign-up with no clear benefit—they're far less likely to engage. The best landing pages create a sense of exclusivity and urgency, making readers feel like they're getting something special that won't be available forever.

Another is a technical issue. If your website takes too much time to load, then people will not stick around. For every second Amazon saves loading the page they make billions of dollars.

Finally, clutter kills conversions. If a page is overwhelming, visually chaotic, or packed with too much information, visitors will get distracted or confused before they even reach the offer. The most effective landing pages are simple, focused, and easy to navigate, guiding the reader toward a single action without unnecessary distractions. I recommend placing your CTA as high on the page as possible, preferably above the scroll if possible.

The good news? All of these problems can be fixed—but only if the author knows they exist. That's where testing comes in. By tracking visitor behavior, authors can optimize their pages for maximum engagement. A landing page isn't a set-it-and-forget-it tool; it's a system that can be refined, improved, and turned into a high-converting asset that works consistently to grow an author's audience and sales.

OPTIMIZING LANDING PAGES WITH HEAT MAPS, SESSION RECORDINGS, AND A/B TESTING

A landing page isn't just a static part of an author's business. It's a living tool that should evolve based on real reader behavior. Many authors set up their landing pages and assume that if they're not converting well, the problem is with their audience or offer. But in reality, most conversion issues come from how the page is structured and how visitors interact with it. The good news is that these problems can be identified and fixed with data-driven insights.

HEAT MAPS: UNDERSTANDING HOW VISITORS ENGAGE WITH A LANDING PAGE

One of the most powerful tools for analyzing reader behavior is a heat map. This tool visually represents where people click, how far they scroll, and where they hesitate or drop off. Instead of guessing what's wrong with a page, heat maps provide a clear picture of how visitors experience it.

For example, if a heat map shows that most visitors never scroll past the halfway point, it means the most important information and call-to-action (CTA) needs to be moved higher on the page. If visitors are clicking on an image instead of the buy button, it signals that the page layout is confusing and needs to be adjusted. If the CTA button isn't getting attention, it might be the wrong color, placed in an ineffective location, or using unconvincing language.

Heat maps take the guesswork out of optimization. Instead of blindly tweaking elements, authors can make targeted changes that directly address how readers interact with the page.

SESSION RECORDINGS: WATCHING HOW READERS NAVIGATE THE PAGE

While heat maps show where visitors are clicking, session recordings reveal how they move through the site in real time. These recordings allow an author to watch as visitors scroll, pause, hover, and navigate, exposing potential roadblocks that might be causing drop-offs.

For example, a session recording might reveal that a visitor hovers over the offer but never clicks the CTA, indicating that the wording isn't compelling enough. Another recording might show a visitor scrolling up and down repeatedly, suggesting they're confused about what to do next. If visitors click away immediately, it could mean that the page lacks a strong hook, failing to capture their interest from the start.

By watching actual reader behavior, authors can pinpoint exactly where visitors lose interest, hesitate, or encounter friction, allowing them to refine the landing page for a smoother, more intuitive experience.

A/B TESTING: EXPERIMENTING TO FIND WHAT WORKS BEST

While heat maps and session recordings diagnose problems, A/B testing helps authors test and refine solutions. A/B testing is the scientific approach to improving a landing page—rather than guessing what will increase conversions, an author tests two different versions of a page and lets real visitor behavior determine the winner.

For example, an author might test two different headlines to see which one keeps visitors on the page longer. They might experiment with two different CTA buttons—one saying "Get Your Special Edition" and another saying "Order Now"—to see which drives more clicks. They could also compare two different offers, such as a discount vs. a bonus chapter, to determine which one leads to more purchases.

A/B testing ensures that every change is backed by data, meaning the landing page is continually improving over time. Instead of making assumptions, authors can see exactly what works and what doesn't, refining their pages to maximize conversions with every test.

The best landing pages aren't just well-written or well-designed—they are optimized based on real visitor behavior. By using heat maps, session recordings, and A/B testing, authors gain deep insights into how readers interact with their pages and can make informed decisions to increase engagement.

Instead of wondering why a page isn't converting, authors who leverage these tools get clear answers and actionable data, allowing them to create a high-performing landing page that guides more readers into their ecosystem, sells more books, and increases revenue over time.

HOW TO APPLY THESE TESTING STRATEGIES TO YOUR LANDING PAGE

By combining heat maps, session recordings, and A/B testing, authors can ensure that their landing page is optimized for real reader behavior.

A simple testing process might look like this:

1. Launch the initial landing page and collect baseline data.
2. Use heat maps to see where readers are engaging (or not).
3. Watch session recordings to identify friction points.
4. Make data-driven improvements (adjusting CTAs, layout, etc.).
5. Run A/B tests to refine messaging, offer structure, and design.
6. Monitor conversions and continue optimizing over time.

Testing isn't a one-time process—it's an ongoing strategy. By continuously refining the page based on real reader behavior, authors can ensure that every backer is guided toward the next step, maximizing long-term engagement and revenue.

WHY YOU NEED (A LOT) OF TRAFFIC TO TEST EFFECTIVELY

One of the most common mistakes authors make when building a series landing page is assuming that any traffic, no matter how small, will give them meaningful insights. Unfortunately, that's not how testing works. If you only have a trickle of visitors—say, a few dozen a week—it's almost impossible to draw reliable conclusions from heat maps, session recordings, or A/B tests. You might see one or two visitors click a button, but that's nowhere near enough data to know if your headline or CTA is truly effective.

- **Statistical Significance**: To confidently say, "Headline A converts better than Headline B," you need a large enough sample size. If only ten people see each version, your findings could be pure luck.

- **Visitor Patterns Vary**: Readers might behave differently on different days of the week, based on their device type, or even the season. More traffic smooths out these fluctuations and gives you clearer insights into what truly works.

Most authors don't actively drive traffic to their landing page beyond a few social media posts or an email blast to their small list. That might deliver short bursts of visitors, but not the consistent flow you need for real-time optimization. Without **steady, substantial** traffic, you'll end up with guesswork instead of data-backed decisions.

HOW TO BOOST YOUR TRAFFIC

- **Leverage Your Existing Audience**: Send regular reminders to your email list, encourage social shares, and link your landing page in your newsletter or pinned posts.
- **Experiment with Ads**: Even a modest ad budget on Facebook, Amazon, or BookBub can bring in new visitors. Paid traffic doesn't just drive immediate sales—it also accelerates your testing.
- **Cross-Promotions**: Team up with authors who write in your genre. You can each promote the other's landing page to your respective audiences, multiplying your reach.
- **Regular Content Updates**: Keep your site or blog fresh. Each new post, excerpt, or behind-the-scenes article can be another reason for people to visit your landing page.

THE BOTTOM LINE

- **Small Traffic** = Good for initial feedback and spotting glaring issues (like broken links).

- **High Traffic** = Essential for meaningful optimization. Without enough visitors, your tests will take forever to produce conclusive results—or worse, lead you to false conclusions.

It may feel like a grind to build and sustain enough traffic, but it's **non-negotiable** if you want to optimize your series landing page properly. In other words, traffic isn't just about making sales; it's about gathering the **data** you need to keep improving your conversion strategy.

BUILDING AN AUTOMATION SEQUENCE FROM TESTED EMAILS

The best way to drive people to a landing page is through an automation sequence.

A well-designed automation sequence helps you nurture new subscribers without manual effort. Each email is automatically sent at the right time, guiding readers toward deeper engagement with your series. The best part? You probably already have most of what you need from your Kickstarter campaign.

1. REUSE PROVEN CONTENT

- **Look at Your Kickstarter Emails:** During your campaign, you likely sent updates, reminders, or stretch-goal announcements. Some performed better than others—higher open rates, more clicks, or more pledges.
- **Identify What Worked:** Pull out the subject lines, calls-to-action, and story snippets that resonated most with backers. These pieces are prime material for your automated welcome or follow-up emails.
- **Adapt, Don't Just Copy-Paste:** Wherever your emails reference pledges or deadlines, swap in calls-to-action that direct readers to your landing page or series buy links. Keep the same tone, style, and compelling hooks.

2. MAP YOUR SEQUENCE

- **Welcome Email**: Immediately thank new subscribers for joining. Introduce them to your series world, referencing the strongest "hook" you found worked during Kickstarter.
- **Follow-Up Emails:** Drip out your best Kickstarter content across several messages—insights into characters or lore, behind-the-scenes tidbits, or personal anecdotes. Each email should include a clear next step (buy the series, watch a trailer, grab bonus content).
- **Final CTA:** Conclude the sequence by encouraging a deeper connection. This might mean purchasing a special edition, joining a membership, or simply staying tuned for more releases.

3. LEVERAGE YOUR KICKSTARTER DATA

- **Open Rate Insights:** The Kickstarter updates that had the highest open rates can become your subject line inspirations. If "Inside the Magic Behind Our Hero's Sword" got a 40% open rate, consider reusing that phrasing in your automated subject lines.
- **Click-Through Patterns:** Which links drew the most clicks—world-building teasers, character art, or limited-time offers? Integrate those same types of links into your automated emails to keep engagement high.
- **Frequency & Timing:** Look at when you sent updates during the campaign. Did morning emails perform better? Did a 3-day reminder drive more pledges? Use those findings to schedule your automation cadence.

4. KEEP TESTING AND REFINING

- **Monitor Performance:** Even though your Kickstarter proved certain emails work, a different audience (or timing) can change the results. Track open rates, click rates, and unsubscribes in your automation software.
- **Tweak and Split Test:** Try variations of your subject lines, email lengths, or CTA wording. Keep building on what resonates most with your current readers.
- **Stay Relevant:** If you add new books or bonus material down the line, update your email sequence accordingly. You want fresh subscribers to see your most current and compelling offers.

You don't have to start from zero when building an automated sequence. Your Kickstarter campaign was already a real-world test of what resonates. By repurposing those proven messages, you can quickly create a powerful, hands-off funnel that nurtures new readers, drives sales, and builds anticipation for whatever you release next. It's all about using data you've already gathered to make every email count.

THE SIDEWAYS SALES LETTER: BREAKING THE PITCH INTO MANAGEABLE CHUNKS

If you don't have Kickstarter emails, or they weren't very good, then there is still hope for you in the sideways sales letter.

A sideways sales letter turns the traditional long form pitch into a series of shorter, more digestible emails. Instead of sending one massive sales email that readers might gloss over, you drip key information across multiple messages, each ending with a link back to your landing page and a reminder that time is running out.

Think of a sideways sales letter as your complete sales page just split into smaller, more digestible pieces. Instead of forcing readers to scroll through a single long pitch (which many will skim or abandon), you present the same material in bite-sized segments over multiple emails or updates.

Why do you need one? Because people don't read things, especially sales things. Modern readers often have limited attention spans. They'll open an email, glance at a few lines, and quickly move on if it feels too long or dense.

Some readers are "skimmers," scanning for key points or interesting subheadings, while others want a more thorough experience but can be put off by endless scrolling. And then there's the issue of "overload aversion": when confronted with a massive block of text, even the most interested potential buyer can feel overwhelmed and simply tune out. Breaking your message into smaller, more digestible pieces helps you engage every type of reader, ensuring that no one feels buried under too much information all at once.

HOW A SIDEWAYS SALES LETTER WORKS

- **Chunk the Content:** Take each main section of your sales page—problem, solution, benefits, testimonials, offer, urgency and turn them into separate, shorter emails.
- **Add a CTA Each Time:** Even though you're revealing the pitch in stages, always include a link or button to buy, sign up, or learn more.

- **Build Momentum:** Each email or segment of the pitch teases the next, creating a sense of anticipation. Rather than one huge pitch, readers get a progressive experience that's easier to follow and less overwhelming.
- **Reinforce Urgency:** As you progress through your series of emails, remind readers that a special offer or deadline is approaching, prompting them to act before time runs out.

Shorter emails or messages are more likely to be read to the end, making them inherently more readable. By dividing your pitch into multiple pieces, you keep each segment focused and digestible, increasing the odds that readers will stick around.

This approach also supports consistent engagement. Instead of hitting your audience with a single, all-encompassing sales pitch, you spread the content out over several days or weeks, offering a steady stream of intrigue and information that keeps people coming back for more. Moreover, multiple touchpoints can lead to higher conversion potential. Each new email provides a fresh angle or deeper insight into your product, giving readers multiple chances to go from "maybe" to "yes."

Finally, it often feels less salesy. Rather than hammering home every detail at once, a sideways approach lets you adopt a more conversational tone and a gradual reveal of benefits. This helps build trust and reduces the off-putting sensation of being "sold to."

A sideways sales letter recognizes that most people won't read a long pitch in one sitting. By dividing your sales message into smaller, strategically sequenced segments, you meet readers where they are—making it more likely they'll absorb the information, stay engaged, and ultimately take action.

Most people think Kickstarters are a huge expenditure of wasted time and energy, but that's only because they aren't utilizing the assets after the campaign. Yes, it's exhausting to do a Kickstarter, but only because setting up marketing assets is exhausting. Most businesses, though, utilize those assets for a long time, which amortizes them over time.

Running a high-energy Kickstarter campaign is really just the beginning, not the finish line. By repurposing the proven copy from your successfully optimized campaign and turning it into a permanent landing page, you create an evergreen funnel that can continue selling your series long after the crowdfunding countdown ends. You don't need a massive e-commerce setup or even new copy—just lift what worked, place it on your own site, and keep refining it with real data.

A single dedicated page, combined with thorough testing (heat maps, session recordings, A/B tests), targeted traffic, and a well-planned email sequence, transforms a fleeting burst of Kickstarter enthusiasm into a long-term revenue engine for your writing career. From enticing headlines to clear CTAs, time-sensitive offers, and sideways sales letters, every piece of this system is designed to guide readers seamlessly from initial interest to purchase—and beyond.

Most importantly, remember that optimization doesn't end once you've transferred your Kickstarter page. It's an ongoing process. Watch how your audience interacts, run experiments, and adjust your approach. Over time, these small, data-driven tweaks compound into a significant boost in conversions and sales—without reinventing the wheel or starting from scratch for each new book.

By combining the live feedback of a Kickstarter campaign with the evergreen power of a dedicated sales funnel, you're building more than a single book launch; you're creating a sustainable growth machine that serves both current fans and future readers. It's the most direct, practical way to keep your series selling itself—day after day, year after year.

THE WEB STORE

For years, authors have been trained to believe that platforms like Amazon, Kobo, Barnes and Noble, Google Play, and Apple Books are the only way to sell books. The logic is simple. Since readers already shop there, the platforms handle the logistics, and sales roll in with minimal effort. It's easy.

But easy doesn't mean smart.

The biggest problem with selling through retailers is that the author doesn't own the customer relationship, the retailer does. Every time a reader buys a book from Amazon, it's Amazon that collects the email address, Amazon that decides which books to recommend next, and Amazon that controls how visible an author's book will be tomorrow. Authors are passengers in someone else's business.

A web store changes that dynamic entirely. Instead of hoping for sales on a third-party platform, authors can own their audience, control their pricing, and build a direct relationship with readers. More importantly, they can offer bundles, special editions, and exclusive perks that aren't possible on Amazon, allowing them to sell fewer books while making more money per reader.

Most authors equate webstores with direct sales, but notice we've only gotten to the traditional webstore now, and I believe it's probably the least important part of the direct sales process unless you are rocking and rolling with your career. Even then, you probably don't have to rely on Shopify when a free Payhip store is 90% as good. It's also the bit I think most authors will make the least on, yet spend the most time worrying about and trying to make work.

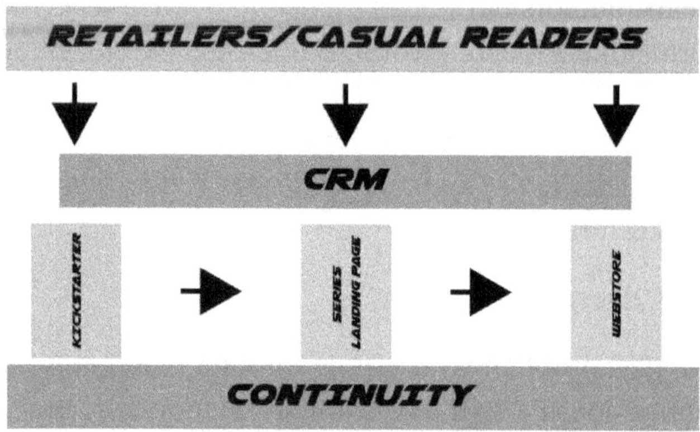

THE PROBLEM WITH RELYING ON RETAILERS

Most authors don't realize how little control they have over their own business until something goes wrong. Maybe their ad costs suddenly spike, making their usual marketing unprofitable. Maybe Amazon tweaks its algorithm, causing their rankings to plummet overnight. Maybe their account gets flagged for reasons beyond their control.

At any moment, an author can lose visibility, revenue, and access to their readers, all because they don't own the customer relationship.

The hard truth is that Amazon's loyalty isn't to authors, it's to its own bottom line. The company will always push its own products first, limit direct communication between authors and readers, and shift policies whenever it benefits their ecosystem.

Authors who rely entirely on retailer sales are always one algorithm change away from losing their income.

A web store is more than just a place to sell books. It's an independent revenue engine that allows authors to:

- Set their own prices and discounts—without worrying about Amazon price-matching or royalty cuts.
- Sell premium products that aren't available on retailers, like collector's editions, signed copies, and exclusive bundles.
- Capture customer emails, allowing for long-term engagement, follow-up sales, and subscriptions.
- Increase average order value by offering bundles and add-ons that encourage bigger purchases.

Most importantly, a web store allows an author to turn a single book sale into an ongoing customer relationship. Instead of selling a $4.99 ebook on Amazon and never hearing from that reader again, an author can sell a $40 hardcover bundle on their store, collect the reader's email, and continue selling to them for years.

Amazon and other retailers restrict how authors can package and sell their books. With a web store, those restrictions disappear. The most successful direct-selling authors don't just offer the same books that are available everywhere else—they create irresistible bundles that can't be found anywhere else. For example:

- **A collector's edition hardcover set** with custom artwork and bonus content.
- **A "series starter" bundle** that includes ebook, audiobook, and behind-the-scenes extras.
- **A premium "fan experience" package** with signed books, merchandise, and an author Q&A session.

These bundles increase revenue per reader while making direct sales the most attractive option for fans.

A decade ago, running an online store would have required custom coding, expensive developers, and a massive time investment. Today, platforms like Shopify, WooCommerce, and Payhip make it easier than ever to set up a store in minutes.

A web store doesn't have to be complicated. The most important thing is having something unique to offer.

Many authors start with one or two bundles, a few signed editions, and an email capture form, then expand as their audience grows. The key isn't to launch with everything, it's to launch with something valuable.

HOW A WEB STORE FITS INTO A BIGGER AUTHOR BUSINESS

A web store isn't a replacement for retailer sales. It's a core piece of an integrated business model that includes retailers. In fact, the more successful you are on retailers, the more successful your webstore will be in the end.

Web stores are the bit of this blueprint second-most reliant on retailer success, the first of which is the retailers themselves. The most successful authors don't abandon Amazon. They use it as a discovery tool while funneling serious fans into their web store. For example:

- A reader buys an ebook on Amazon → The backmatter directs them to a web store for a special bundle.

- A Kickstarter backer supports a campaign → The fulfillment email includes a link to exclusive store offers.
- A retailer reader finishes Book One → They're offered a direct sales discount for Book Two.

By positioning the web store as the premium, high-value experience, authors maximize revenue while keeping a foothold in other sales channels.

HOW TO BUILD A HIGH-CONVERTING WEB STORE

A web store isn't just a place to sell books. It's the gateway to a direct relationship with readers. Subscriptions are an undercurrent, landing pages are often hidden, and Kickstarters are time-bound, which makes the web store the most visible part of your direct sales brand.

Unlike Amazon, where an author has no control over the buying experience, a web store allows for premium offers, special editions, and unique bundles that maximize revenue per customer, but simply having a store isn't enough. Many authors set up a Shopify or WooCommerce site, add a few books, and expect readers to buy. They don't realize that a store must be designed to guide the reader toward a purchase, just like a well-structured book guides a reader through a story.

A high-converting web store isn't about throwing up product listings and hoping for sales. It's about creating an experience that makes readers excited to buy, feel like insiders, and eager to return.

WHY A WEB STORE IS MORE THAN JUST A PRODUCT LIST

Amazon has conditioned readers to expect a certain type of buying experience—simple, fast, and impersonal. If an author's web store looks and feels just like another Amazon page, readers will default back to Amazon out of habit.

A direct sales store has to feel different. It needs to offer something Amazon can't—an exclusive, premium buying experience that feels special and exciting.

Readers should land on an author's store and immediately see the value of buying direct. The experience should make them think, *Why would I buy anywhere else?*

Every successful author store is **built on three essential pages**:

1. A HOMEPAGE THAT HOOKS READERS IMMEDIATELY

The homepage isn't just a **starting point**. It's a **sales pitch**. It should instantly communicate:

- **What makes this store different** (collector's editions, signed books, exclusive content).
- **A clear next step** (buy now, claim a special offer, join a VIP membership).
- **Social proof** (bestseller badges, reader testimonials, or reviews).

Instead of a simple product grid, the homepage should feel like a curated experience. The goal is to make the reader excited to explore.

2. A PRODUCT PAGE THAT SELLS THE EXPERIENCE, NOT JUST THE BOOK

Most authors make the mistake of treating product pages like Amazon listings—just a title, description, and price. But on a direct sales store, a product page needs to sell an experience, not just a book.

A high-converting product page includes:

- **Multiple images**—not just the cover, but angled shots, lifestyle photos, and packaging previews.
- **Compelling copy**—instead of *"Hardcover edition, 300 pages"*, use *"A beautifully crafted hardcover edition with exclusive author notes and a custom bookplate."*
- **Upsell options**—"Upgrade to the Signed Collector's Bundle for Just $15 More!"

Readers should feel like they're buying something unique and valuable, not just ordering another book.

3. A CHECKOUT PAGE THAT REDUCES FRICTION

A complicated checkout process kills conversions. If a reader has to jump through hoops to complete their purchase, they'll abandon their cart.

A high-converting checkout page should:

- **Offer guest checkout**—forcing account creation increases drop-offs.
- **Provide multiple payment options**—credit cards, PayPal, Buy Now Pay Later.
- **Minimize unnecessary fields**—only ask for what's essential to complete the purchase.

The goal is to make buying **as smooth as possible**, so the reader doesn't have time to reconsider.

EXCLUSIVE BUNDLES: THE ULTIMATE DIFFERENTIATOR

While special editions and signed copies can set your store apart, exclusive bundles are the real game-changer. Bundles combine multiple items like different formats of your book, artwork, digital extras, or even personalized notes into a single, premium package readers can't get anywhere else. They're a clear signal that your store isn't just another retail portal; it's an experience. Why does this work?

1. **Higher Per-Order Value:** Offering a bundle that includes a signed hardcover, an ebook, and a limited-edition art print can significantly raise your average order value. Even if a reader initially plans to spend $15, a compelling bundle could convince them to spend $50 or more because they see a clear boost in value.

2. **Scarcity and Exclusivity:** When you label something a "Collector's Bundle" or "Limited Edition Box Set," readers know they won't find it on Amazon or in a typical bookstore. This exclusivity both justifies a higher price and taps into the fear of missing out.

3. **Built-In Opportunity for Fan Engagement:** Bundles aren't just about the physical product; you can include digital perks like bonus short stories, behind-the-scenes videos, or invitations to private author Q&A sessions. These extras create a deeper, more personal connection between you and your readers—turning casual buyers into dedicated fans.

4. **Easier Marketing:** Bundles are inherently newsworthy. They give you something special to talk about in emails, social media posts, and ads.

Highlighting limited availability or a ticking countdown for orders can spur readers to act quickly, rather than "thinking about it" and forgetting later.

TIPS FOR CRAFTING IRRESISTIBLE BUNDLES

- **Theme Your Bundles**: For instance, a "World-Building Bundle" might include annotated maps, digital lore guides, or exclusive behind-the-scenes notes on how the series was created.
- **Offer Tiered Options**: Allow fans to pick between a basic bundle (signed paperback + ebook) and a deluxe version (hardcover + extras + personal note). This covers both budget-conscious readers and superfans who want the works.
- **Keep It Limited**: If everything's always available, you lose that exclusivity factor. Time-limited or quantity-limited bundles drive urgency and encourage immediate purchases.

A web store that sells exclusive bundles and curated experiences can't be duplicated on Amazon or any other standard retailer. By offering something genuinely special, you give readers a powerful reason to buy direct and to keep coming back for new releases or seasonal specials. It's your chance to stand out from the automated, one-click norm and truly connect with your audience on a personal (and profitable) level.

WHY CONVERSION MATTERS MORE THAN TRAFFIC IN A WEB STORE

A common misconception among authors launching a web store is that more visitors will automatically lead to more sales. But most web stores don't fail because of a traffic problem. They fail because of a conversion problem. An author could drive thousands of visitors to their site, but if those visitors aren't converting into paying customers, the traffic is meaningless. Instead of focusing on bringing in more people, a high-performing web store increases revenue by getting more value out of each visitor.

One of the biggest advantages of selling direct is the freedom to bundle and upsell products in ways that retailers like Amazon don't allow. This is where smart pricing strategies become essential. Instead of just offering single-book purchases, successful web store owners maximize the value of every transaction by presenting readers with compelling bundles and upsells that encourage larger purchases.

For example, rather than selling a single hardcover for $25, an author can offer a signed collector's bundle for $50, including exclusive artwork, a bookplate, and bonus content. Instead of simply listing an ebook on its own, they can package it with an audiobook and exclusive short story for $40. A reader who enjoys a series can be guided toward a "complete series" set at a discount, encouraging them to binge-read the entire collection rather than buying books one at a time.

Authors who use bundles and strategic pricing often sell fewer books in terms of raw volume but make significantly more per reader, increasing their overall revenue without needing to constantly chase more customers.

Beyond bundles, one of the simplest yet most effective ways to boost revenue is by adding an upsell at checkout. When a reader is already in the process of making a purchase, they are far more likely to say yes to a small, relevant add-on. A well-placed upsell prompt can increase revenue by 20–30%, making it one of the highest-impact changes an author can make to their store.

For example, right before checkout is completed, the store could offer:

- "Before you complete your purchase, add a signed bookplate for just $5!"
- "Upgrade to the exclusive Kickstarter edition—only 50 copies left!"

These small, last-minute incentives don't require additional traffic. They simply encourage visitors who are already buying to spend a little more. If you can double the customers' spend, you can make the same money from the same number of customers.

A web store doesn't succeed by just getting more people to visit. It succeeds by maximizing every reader's experience, increasing their purchase value, and ensuring that every transaction brings in as much revenue as possible. By focusing on bundles, upsells, and strategic pricing, authors can dramatically increase their store's profitability without needing to attract more visitors.

Cross-selling is another powerful way to increase revenue by recommending complementary products that enhance the reader's purchase. Instead of waiting until checkout, cross-sells are introduced earlier in the shopping experience, guiding readers to discover additional books or merchandise they might love.

For example, if a reader adds Book One of a series to their cart, they might see:

- "Complete the adventure—grab Books Two and Three at a special bundle price!"
- "Love this world? Get the companion novella featuring your favorite side character."

Cross-sells work because they feel natural and helpful rather than intrusive. They tap into the reader's existing interest and present an opportunity to enhance their experience, making them far more likely to add more to their order.

Not every visitor is ready to commit to a premium bundle or high-ticket item. This is where down-sells come into play by offering a lower-priced alternative to keep the sale rather than losing it altogether.

For example, if a reader clicks away from a deluxe signed edition, a down-sell might offer:

- "Not ready for the hardcover? Get the ebook and audiobook bundle instead!"
- "The collector's edition isn't for you? Grab the standard edition for half the price."

A well-executed down-sell keeps the transaction alive, ensuring that even hesitant buyers convert rather than abandon their cart. Instead of losing a sale entirely, the author recaptures revenue while still delivering value to the reader.

A web store doesn't succeed by just getting more people to visit. It succeeds by maximizing every reader's experience, increasing their purchase value, and ensuring that every transaction brings in as much revenue as possible.

By strategically implementing:

- **Bundles**, which increase **average order value** by combining products.
- **Upsells**, which add **premium extras** at checkout.
- **Cross-sells**, which introduce **related products** to enhance the purchase.
- **Down-sells**, which **save sales** that might otherwise be lost.

Authors can dramatically increase their store's profitability without needing to attract more visitors. A well-structured store doesn't just sell books, it creates a seamless shopping experience where every reader has an easy, enticing path to buying more.

Readers don't just buy books, they buy experiences, exclusiveness, and the feeling of being part of something special.

That's why Amazon-style product listings don't work for most authors. Yes, if you make Amazon-friendly books, then maybe mimicking that style will work for a while, but the best-selling author stores make the shopping experience feel personal, premium, and exclusive.

Amazon trains readers to think, *"I can always buy this later."* A well-designed web store creates urgency by making the offer feel unique, limited, and special. You can do this by:

- Use countdown timers on limited time offers.
- Show remaining stock ("Only 10 copies left!").
- Create special editions that won't be available again.

When a reader knows this book won't be available on Amazon, and it might sell out, they act immediately.

HOW TO DRIVE TRAFFIC TO A WEB STORE (WITHOUT OVERSPENDING ON ADS)

A well-built web store is useless if no one visits it. Unlike Amazon, which has built-in traffic from readers browsing for books, a web store requires a deliberate strategy to bring in potential buyers. But the goal isn't just traffic for the sake of traffic. It's about attracting the right readers, engaging them, and turning them into repeat customers.

Many authors assume that running ads is the only way to get traffic, but the best web stores thrive on a mix of Kickstarter backers, retailer conversions, and targeted ad traffic that brings in buyers, not just browsers.

Traffic isn't just about numbers. Many authors focus on getting people to their store, assuming that if enough visitors arrive, sales will follow. But traffic alone doesn't guarantee conversions. A high-performing store isn't just about bringing people in, it's about turning them into paying customers. Without a clear strategy for conversion, most visitors will browse, leave, and never return.

One of the most common mistakes authors make is sending traffic to a generic homepage instead of a targeted landing page. A homepage is often cluttered with multiple navigation options, distracting readers from taking immediate action. A well-designed landing page, on the other hand, is built for conversion, focusing on one specific offer with a compelling call to action. Instead of letting visitors wander, a landing page guides them toward a single, clear decision whether that's buying a special edition, joining a subscription, or signing up for a pre-order.

Even if an author sends traffic to the right page, another major mistake is not giving readers a reason to buy now. If there's no urgency, exclusivity, or limited-time offer, many visitors will think, *I'll come back later*—but they won't. Strong web stores use scarcity and incentives to encourage immediate action. Whether it's a limited stock warning, an exclusive pre-order bonus, or a "launch-week discount," giving visitors a reason to act right now increases conversions dramatically.

HOW TO USE KICKSTARTER AS A WEB STORE TRAFFIC ENGINE

Kickstarter is one of the most underutilized traffic sources for web stores. Backers already trust the author and have proven they're willing to pay premium prices for books. But most authors don't have a system to transition them into web store customers.

A successful Kickstarter doesn't just fund a book. It creates an audience of buyers who are primed for future offers. Here's how to do it.

1. **Post-Campaign Emails That Lead to Exclusive Offers**
    a. Instead of just sending a "thank you" email after fulfillment, direct backers to **a web store landing page** with a **Kickstarter-only offer** (limited-time discounts, signed editions, or exclusive bundles).
2. **Using Fulfillment Updates to Funnel Backers into the Store**

a. Every Kickstarter update should **mention the web store**: *"Want more from this series? Get exclusive editions at my store!"*

b. Backers who didn't grab certain rewards during the campaign will often **buy them later if given the chance.**

3. **Upsell Kickstarter Backers into Memberships & Subscriptions**

a. Offer a **Kickstarter-only membership level** that gives backers early access to future books.

b. Use fulfillment emails to invite them into **a private reader community**—which can later be monetized through direct sales.

HOW TO CONVERT RETAILER READERS INTO DIRECT CUSTOMERS

Amazon, Kobo, Google Play, Barnes and Noble, and Apple Books sell a lot of books, but they don't help authors build direct customer relationships. However, a reader who buys on Amazon can still be turned into a web store buyer, if they're given the right incentive.

The best way to do this? Leverage the backmatter of every book to drive readers to an exclusive direct-sales offer. How to funnel retailer readers to a web store.

1. **Use Backmatter to Offer an Exclusive Web Store Deal**

a. Instead of a generic "Join my newsletter" link, include: *"Get an exclusive signed edition & bonus short story—only available in my store!"*

2. **Run Special Promotions for Retailer Buyers**

    a. Example: *"If you bought Book One on Amazon, get Book Two at 20% off—only on my store."*

    b. Creates **urgency and exclusivity**, making readers more likely to buy direct instead of waiting for an Amazon discount.

3. **Bundle Direct Sales Offers with Retailer Sales**

    a. Example: *"Bought the ebook on Amazon? Upgrade to the signed hardcover bundle on my store for just $30 more."*

    b. Encourages retailer buyers to **spend more on direct sales.**

Retailer readers aren't lost customers, they're potential direct buyers if the right funnel is in place.

HOW TO USE PAID ADS PROFITABLY FOR WEB STORE TRAFFIC

Paid ads can be a powerful tool for direct sales, but only when used strategically. Many authors run ads with the hope that any traffic will convert into sales, only to see clicks that don't turn into purchases and ad costs that outweigh profits. Without a clear targeted approach, paid ads can quickly become a waste of money rather than a reliable growth strategy.

To make ads profitable, an author must ensure that every visitor is sent to a high-converting landing page, not a generic store homepage. A **store homepage** is designed for browsing, but an ad needs to lead visitors directly to an offer that makes it easy to buy. A **dedicated landing page** with one focused product, a clear call-to-action, and a sense of urgency significantly increases conversions.

Equally important is what's being advertised. Running ads to low-value products like a single ebook or a standard paperback is a recipe for failure. Ads work best when driving traffic to high-value offers that maximize the revenue per customer, such as signed editions, premium hardcovers, and first-in-series bundles. When the average order value is higher, ad spend becomes much more sustainable.

Even with a great product and a well-optimized landing page, most visitors won't buy the first time they visit a store. That's why retargeting ads are essential. These ads target people who visited the store but didn't purchase, bringing them back with a reminder, an exclusive discount, or a time-sensitive offer. Retargeting ensures that the money spent on initial traffic doesn't go to waste, increasing the likelihood of conversion over time.

Not every product is worth running ads for. Some products naturally convert at a higher rate, while others struggle to justify the ad spend.

Best Products to Advertise for Direct Sales

- **Exclusive signed editions** → Creates urgency and scarcity, increasing conversion rates.
- **First-in-series bundles** → Higher order values help cover ad costs, making sales more profitable.
- **Collector's editions with premium pricing** → Maximizes revenue per customer, ensuring ad spend generates strong returns.

Worst Products to Advertise for Direct Sales

- **Single ebooks under $5** → Ad costs will often exceed the profit, making them unviable.

- **Standard paperbacks available on Amazon** → If a book can be purchased on a major retailer, readers will often default to that option, reducing direct conversions.
- **Books without a follow-up offer** → If there's no subscription, bundle, or future book promotion, one-time buyers provide little long-term value.

AUTOMATING THE WEB STORE FOR LONG-TERM SUCCESS

For many authors, the dream of selling direct sounds amazing—higher revenue per sale, complete control over pricing, and the ability to build long-term reader relationships. But the reality? Maintaining a web store can feel overwhelming if every sale, email, and customer interaction requires manual effort.

The solution? Automation.

A well-built web store should be a self-sustaining revenue engine, not a constant source of stress. The most successful direct-selling authors aren't manually tracking every customer or sending individual follow-up emails; they use pre-built systems that run in the background, keeping sales flowing even while they're writing.

This final section will explore how to automate key parts of the web store—from abandoned cart recovery and post-purchase upsells to VIP customer rewards and evergreen sales funnels. By the end, an author will have a clear plan for turning their store into a passive income machine that generates sales 24/7.

WHY MANUAL WEB STORES DON'T SCALE (AND WHY AUTOMATION DOES)

A web store operates very differently from Amazon. On Amazon, readers browse, discover a book through search or recommendations, and make a purchase—all without the author's involvement. The retailer handles everything: sales processing, delivery, and even follow-up recommendations to encourage future purchases. But a web store doesn't have Amazon's built-in traffic or automated sales system, which means it requires a more direct and proactive approach to keep sales flowing.

Without automation, managing a web store quickly becomes overwhelming. An author might find themselves manually sending follow-up emails to every new customer, trying to nurture relationships but spending valuable time on repetitive tasks. They might struggle to track which readers have already purchased, leading to awkward duplicate promotions or missed upsell opportunities. And they could find themselves constantly pushing sales, running social media promotions or discount campaigns just to keep traffic coming in.

At first, this level of manual involvement seems manageable. With a small audience, an author can respond to individual buyers, personally thank new customers, and keep track of their store activity. But as the audience grows, this approach doesn't scale. An author with hundreds or thousands of customers can't manually follow up with each one, remember every buyer's history, or continuously generate new sales without burning out.

This is why automation isn't just helpful, it's essential. With the right systems in place, a web store can run efficiently with minimal hands-on effort, allowing the author to focus on writing and creating rather than managing sales logistics. Automated email sequences ensure that every new buyer receives a personalized welcome and follow-up offers. Cart recovery emails bring back potential customers who didn't complete their purchase. Upsell and cross-sell automations increase the average order value without requiring additional marketing.

Instead of struggling to maintain sales manually, authors who integrate smart automation into their web store create a scalable, self-sustaining system—one that doesn't just generate revenue, but does so consistently and efficiently, without constant oversight.

The best part? You don't even have to do it. There are people all over the publishing landscape from VAs to COO-level implementers who can do this work for you on everything from visualization to set-up and maintenance.

HOW TO AUTOMATE KEY WEB STORE SYSTEMS

There are three core areas where automation can dramatically **increase revenue and save time**:

1. Recovering Lost Sales with Abandoned Cart Emails
2. Boosting Revenue Per Sale with Upsells & Cross-Sells
3. Building Long-Term Customer Loyalty with VIP Rewards

Each of these ensures that more visitors become buyers, more buyers spend more per order, and more customers come back for future purchases.

1. RECOVERING LOST SALES WITH ABANDONED CART EMAILS

The average e-commerce store loses **70% of potential sales** to cart abandonment. Readers add a book to their cart, get distracted, and never return. But what if the store **automatically reminded them to complete their purchase?**

The best abandoned cart sequences send **three automated emails**:

- **Email #1 (One Hour After Abandonment) – "You Left Something Behind"**
    - A friendly reminder with a direct link back to their cart.
- **Email #2 (24 Hours Later) – "Your Special Offer is Expiring"**
    - Creates urgency by offering **a limited-time discount or bonus**.
- **Email #3 (48 Hours Later) – "Final Call: Last Chance to Claim Your Book"**
    - A last attempt to bring them back before the deal disappears.

Why it works: Readers often need a simple nudge to follow through on a purchase. Automated reminders bring them back without manual effort.

2. BOOSTING REVENUE PER SALE WITH UPSELLS & CROSS-SELLS

Once a reader is in **buying mode**, they are **more likely to buy additional items**, but only if they're presented with a **compelling offer at the right moment**.

How to Automate Upsells & Cross-Sells in a Web Store

1. **Post-Purchase Upsells (After Checkout, Before They Leave)**
   a. Example: *"Wait! Add the signed hardcover for just $10 more!"*
   b. **Why it works:** Readers who **just bought** are **most likely to upgrade.**
2. **Cross-Sells (During Checkout)**
   a. Example: *"Bundle this book with the exclusive audiobook for 20% off!"*
   b. **Why it works: Higher perceived value** encourages **larger purchases.**
3. **One-Click Upsells (Immediately After Purchase)**
   a. Example: *"Your order is confirmed—want to add Book Two for 50% off?"*
   b. **Why it works:** The reader **already has their credit card out**—they're in a **buying mindset.**

Why it works: Readers love a good deal, and upsells increase revenue per customer without increasing ad costs.

3. BUILDING LONG-TERM CUSTOMER LOYALTY WITH VIP REWARDS

One-time buyers are great, but repeat customers are where the real profits are. A store that automatically rewards loyal customers will always outperform a store that only focuses on new buyers. Sometimes, you can do this through integrations with your store, and others need to be done in your email provider. I have a very simple one set up in my email provider.

How to Automate a VIP Rewards Program

1. **Create a "Superfan" Tier for Repeat Customers**

    a. Example: *"Spend $100 in my store and unlock VIP pricing for life!"*
    b. **Why it works:** Encourages readers to **keep buying** to reach VIP status.
2. **Offer Loyalty Discounts for Second-Time Buyers**
    a. Example: *"Since you bought Book One, here's a private discount for Book Two."*
    b. **Why it works:** A targeted offer keeps them **moving through the series**.
3. **Send Personalized Anniversary Offers**
    a. Example: *"You've been a customer for a year— here's an exclusive signed edition just for VIPs!"*
    b. **Why it works:** Makes customers **feel appreciated**, increasing long-term retention.

Why it works: Readers love to feel like insiders. A simple VIP program makes them want to stay engaged with the store.

A successful direct-sales web store isn't about constantly pushing promotions or manually managing every sale. It's about building a system that works in the background, turning visitors into buyers, buyers into repeat customers, and repeat customers into loyal superfans—all without requiring the author's daily involvement.

A fully optimized, automated store should recover lost sales, increase order value, and encourage long-term engagement. Abandoned cart emails ensure that potential buyers who left without completing their purchase get a second chance to return. Post-purchase upsells offer additional products at checkout, increasing the value of each order. A VIP rewards program nurtures reader loyalty, giving customers a reason to return for future purchases.

And automated email sequences keep readers engaged, providing timely reminders, special offers, and incentives to bring them back to the store.

Each of these elements works together to ensure that every visitor has multiple opportunities to convert, spend more, and stay engaged—without requiring the author to manually follow up or constantly promote their store.

A direct-sales web store should feel like a business that runs itself—bringing in revenue, nurturing reader relationships, and ensuring steady growth without the author needing to constantly push for sales. Instead of chasing one-time buyers, a well-structured system guides customers through an ongoing experience, ensuring that every purchase is just the beginning of a long-term relationship.

With the right automation in place, authors can:

- **Spend more time writing** instead of constantly selling.
- **Generate passive income** through repeat buyers.
- **Create a thriving reader community** that returns for every book.

Selling direct isn't just about getting off Amazon. It's about building a scalable, long-term business that puts the author in control. Instead of being dependent on retailer algorithms, ad costs, or unpredictable marketplace shifts, direct-sales authors create a stable foundation where their income, audience, and creative freedom are entirely their own.

HOW EACH SALES CHANNEL FITS INTO THE BIGGER SYSTEM

A successful author business isn't built on just one platform. It's a system where every sales channel plays a role. The best authors don't just use Kickstarter, web stores, or retailer sales in isolation. They make each sale feed into the next, creating an ecosystem where every reader moves deeper into engagement.

Most authors start by focusing on one platform at a time, which is good for overwhelm, but the real power comes when Kickstarter, retailers, subscriptions, landing pages, and web stores work together. Instead of seeing these as separate strategies, authors who succeed in direct sales connect them into a seamless experience for their readers.

This section will break down how each sales channel fits into a long-term business strategy, ensuring that every campaign, every launch, and every new book fuels the next.

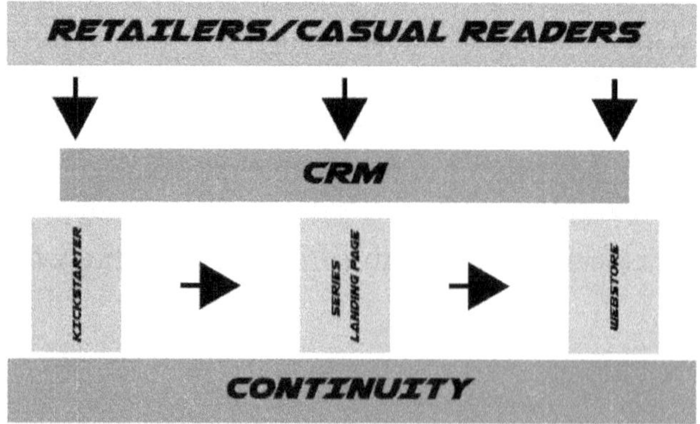

THE ROLE OF CONTINUITY: TURNING ONE-TIME BUYERS INTO SUBSCRIBERS

The most successful authors don't just aim for individual purchases. They design their business so that each sale naturally guides readers toward ongoing support. This is where continuity—subscriptions, memberships, or other recurring revenue models—becomes invaluable. Once a reader finishes your book, a continuity program gives them a reason to stay invested in your world, month after month or year after year, rather than drifting away.

In a market that often swings between feast and famine, offering subscribers or members a reason to pay you regularly can smooth out your cash flow and free you from the anxiety of "launch-or-starve." Subscriptions and memberships also deepen engagement by keeping readers actively involved in your universe. Whether you provide them with exclusive chapters, behind-the-scenes content, or interactive Q&A sessions, the simple act of showing up month after month creates a stronger emotional bond that often turns casual supporters into enthusiastic evangelists for your work. And when the time comes to launch a new book, you already have a ready-made audience of subscribers who are primed to buy on day one, sparing you the scramble of having to rustle up interest from scratch.

However, subscriptions take forever to pay off, which means they should be the undercurrent of your publishing business. Every time you have a launch, or post something, your subscription is building little by little, until it becomes a juggernaut.

KICKSTARTER: THE BEST WAY TO FUND AND TEST NEW PRODUCTS

Kickstarter isn't just a way to fund a book. It's the first step in your publishing business. A well-executed campaign doesn't just generate cash upfront; it builds an engaged audience of backers who are primed for future sales. Instead of treating Kickstarter as a one-time event, successful direct-selling authors use it as the first step in a larger system that fuels long-term growth.

Kickstarter serves four critical functions. First, it provides upfront funding, eliminating financial risk by covering production costs before the book is even printed. Instead of paying out-of-pocket and hoping for future sales, authors can confidently invest in premium editions, special packaging, and marketing knowing the demand is already there.

Second, it acts as a high-profile launch event, generating excitement and momentum long before the book reaches retailer shelves or web stores. The built-in urgency of a Kickstarter campaign drives engagement in a way that traditional launches often struggle to achieve.

Third, it allows a testing ground to develop new products and marketing messaging, so you leave your campaign with a tightly designed message that works, and that you can carry over to the rest of your business.

Finally, and most importantly, Kickstarter creates a loyal base of readers who are more likely to buy direct in the future. Unlike casual retail buyers, backers have actively chosen to support an author's work before it's available, making them far more likely to continue purchasing through the author's ecosystem.

RETAILERS: WHY AMAZON STILL PLAYS A ROLE IN DIRECT SALES

Many direct-selling authors are tempted to abandon Amazon and other retailers entirely, believing that direct sales alone are the key to success, but ditching retailers completely is a mistake. Platforms like Amazon, Kobo, Barnes & Noble, Google Play, and Apple still play a crucial role not as primary sales channels, but as discoverability tools. The key isn't to avoid retailers; it's to use them strategically to funnel readers into a direct sales ecosystem.

Retailers offer one major advantage that direct sales alone can't match: built-in traffic. Discoverability is one of the biggest challenges in direct sales, and retailer platforms introduce new readers to an author's work through organic search, category rankings, and recommendation algorithms. A book with steady sales on Amazon doesn't just make money, it builds algorithmic momentum, which increases visibility, leading to more organic sales without additional effort.

Beyond visibility, retailers also serve as a low-friction entry point for readers. Many customers still prefer to buy on Amazon first, either because they trust the platform, have Kindle Unlimited subscriptions, or want instant access to ebooks. Expecting all readers to immediately shift to a web store isn't realistic, but what happens after that first retailer sale is entirely within the author's control.

The most successful direct-selling authors don't abandon retailers, they leverage them. A well-optimized retailer presence feeds into a web store, a subscription, or a Kickstarter. Instead of chasing rankings for the sake of rankings, these authors turn retailer visibility into long-term, high-value customer relationships that fuel their business far beyond a single book sale.

LANDING PAGES: THE MISSING LINK THAT GUIDES READERS TO THE RIGHT OFFER

Most authors make the mistake of sending readers straight to a store homepage, assuming they'll browse and find something to buy. But a homepage is not a sales funnel. It's a general entry point, often cluttered with multiple navigation options, different products, and distractions that reduce conversions. A visitor who lands on a homepage without clear direction is far more likely to leave than to make a purchase.

A landing page, on the other hand, is designed for one specific action. Instead of presenting multiple choices, it guides readers toward a single, focused decision, whether that's buying a bundle, claiming a discount, or signing up for a subscription. A well-optimized landing page removes distractions and ensures that every visitor sees the right offer at the right time, increasing the likelihood of conversion.

The most successful authors don't just drive traffic, they guide it into a structured funnel. Different types of landing pages serve different functions, but all are designed to capture a reader's attention and make taking action as easy as possible.

A well-designed landing page ensures that every visitor has a direct, frictionless path toward making a purchase. Whether it's converting Kickstarter backers into long-term customers, guiding retailer readers into direct sales, or optimizing ad traffic for maximum ROI, landing pages turn casual visitors into paying customers at a much higher rate than a generic homepage ever could.

Instead of hoping visitors will explore and find something they want, authors who use landing pages guide their audience to the right offer at the right time ensuring higher conversions, better sales, and a more efficient direct sales strategy.

WEB STORES: THE HOME FOR HIGH-MARGIN, DIRECT SALES

A web store isn't just a place where books are sold, it's where an author's most valuable customers buy. Unlike retailer platforms, where purchases are often driven by convenience, a web store attracts superfans—readers who are willing to invest in premium products, exclusive editions, and long-term engagement with the author.

Unlike Amazon, where books are priced for mass-market appeal, a web store allows for premium pricing, enabling authors to generate significantly higher revenue per customer. Instead of selling a single ebook for $4.99 and earning a fraction of that in royalties, an author can offer signed editions, deluxe hardcovers, and collector's bundles, increasing the average order value. Readers who buy direct aren't just looking for the cheapest option. They want special editions, exclusive perks, and a direct connection to the author.

A web store isn't a standalone tool—it works best when fully integrated into an author's larger business model. It functions as the central hub where the most engaged readers come to buy, but those readers must first be guided from Kickstarter, retailer sales, and email marketing into direct sales channels.

The difference between a struggling web store and a thriving one isn't just having a store. It's creating a system where readers are continuously moving through the ecosystem, deepening their engagement, and returning for future purchases. When every piece of the business works together, the web store becomes a sustainable, high-revenue engine that fuels an author's long-term success.

CONVENTIONS AND SIGNING EVENTS: THE (NOT SO) SECRET SIXTH STEP

Conventions and signing events might not be an official part of this framework, but they deserve a place in the conversation. Think of them as a hybrid between your webstore and retail sales. How you use them determines whether they act like a cash register, a lead magnet, or both.

- **Grow your audience.** Give away freebies for mailing list sign-ups or offer low-cost incentives that make it easy for new readers to step into your ecosystem.

- **Move inventory.** Bundle and sell your extra stock at a discount, or create exclusive editions that can only be bought in person.
- **Treat it like advertising.** Don't forget to account for table costs and travel like you would any marketing budget. The return isn't just sales. It's exposure, leads, and long-term readers.

Before I retired from doing conventions, they acted as all this for me. I didn't have a webstore for years and years. It was only teaching web stores in our Direct Sales Launchpad course that forced me to build one out of shame.

Most of my books weren't even on retailers until recently because I was meeting so many new, casual fans at conventions that I could give them a better (and more profitable) experience offering books exclusively in my own ecosystem.

I still use writing conferences as a great way to network and plan strategic partnerships with writers, editors, agents, and publishers.

Handled correctly, conventions and signing events can be more than just selling books in person. They become an extension of your ecosystem, giving you both visibility and momentum you can't always get online.

BRINGING IT ALL TOGETHER: THE SALES FUNNEL IN ACTION

A successful author business isn't just about selling books. It's about creating a system where every sale fuels the next, ensuring ongoing revenue, reader engagement, and business sustainability. Instead of relying on one-off launches or isolated sales channels, the most effective direct-selling authors integrate Kickstarter, retailers, landing pages, and a web store into a seamless ecosystem.

Kickstarter serves as the first step, generating upfront revenue while introducing backers to the author's direct sales platform. A well-structured campaign doesn't just fund a book, it creates long-term customers. After the campaign, backers should be guided toward the web store, where they can purchase additional books, sign up for exclusive memberships, or access limited time offers.

Retailer sales remain a valuable discovery tool, but instead of treating them as standalone transactions, direct-selling authors use backmatter strategically to funnel retailer readers into direct sales offers. A well-placed call-to-action, offering a bonus novella, exclusive discount, or signed hardcover, moves casual buyers into the author's direct ecosystem—turning a one-time Amazon sale into a long-term customer relationship.

Landing pages play a critical role in capturing reader interest and converting traffic into direct sales. Instead of sending ad traffic or email subscribers to a generic homepage, targeted landing pages present a clear offer— whether that's a special bundle, VIP membership, or exclusive pre-order—making it easy for readers to take immediate action.

Then a web store becomes the front-facing part of your author brand, even if they aren't making as much money as the other bits. Unlike retailer platforms, where pricing, data, and customer relationships are controlled by third parties, a direct sales store allows authors to sell premium editions and create exclusive bundles maximizing revenue and deepening reader engagement.

Meanwhile, a subscription undergirds it all, slowly building over time while you don't need it until it becomes a powerful driver of revenue stabilizing your business. Subscriptions ensure financial stability in a way that one-time purchases never can. Readers who love an author's work often want more than just the occasional book release. A subscription gives them a reason to stay engaged, offering early access to new stories, behind-the-scenes content, or exclusive editions that aren't available anywhere else. More importantly, subscriptions create continuity in revenue, allowing an author to build a financial foundation that isn't dependent on individual book launches.

Each channel feeds into the next, creating continuity, momentum, and long-term revenue. Instead of constantly chasing new readers, direct-selling authors build an ccosystem where every sale strengthens the business, ensuring sustainable growth and financial independence.

LAUNCHING BOOKS FOR FUN AND PROFIT

For years, Kindle Unlimited (KU) was one of the most appealing programs for indie authors. The promise was simple: readers could borrow books through Amazon's subscription service, and authors would get paid based on how many pages were read. It seemed like a win-win with unlimited books for readers and a steady income for authors. But as the market evolved, so did KU's limitations.

Payouts have steadily decreased, with each page read earning less than they did in previous years. What once provided a solid income for authors relying on high-read-through series is now a shrinking piece of the pie. With more authors in the program, the overall KU fund is split among a larger group, meaning even if you're doing everything right—writing bingeable books, optimizing for KU readers, and staying exclusive to Amazon—you're still making less per page than before.

At the same time, alternative platforms are rising, giving authors new ways to make money outside of Amazon's ecosystem. Kickstarter, Ream, and Patreon have proven that readers are willing to pay directly for content whether it's through limited edition print runs, exclusive serialized fiction, or ongoing memberships. These platforms offer something KU doesn't: control. Instead of relying on Amazon's fluctuating payout rates and unpredictable algorithm shifts, authors can build direct relationships with their audience and earn predictable, stable revenue.

And that's the big shift: Amazon is no longer the only game in town. For years, KU felt like the default option for indie authors, especially those writing in genres that thrived in the subscription model. But now, more authors are going wide, distributing their books on multiple platforms rather than remaining locked into Amazon's exclusivity. They're discovering that Kobo, Apple Books, Barnes and Noble, and Google Play, along with direct sales through Shopify or Kickstarter offer them more flexibility and often higher profits per sale than KU ever did.

That doesn't mean KU is dead. It still has a place, especially for authors who know how to maximize read-through and keep readers engaged in long series. But it's no longer the automatic best choice for indie publishing. The landscape is shifting, and the most successful authors are the ones adapting, leveraging KU where it makes sense while exploring new opportunities that offer greater financial stability.

For authors who have built their entire business around KU, this shift can feel unsettling. But the truth is, diversification is power. Relying on a single platform, especially one that can change its payout structure at any time, is a risky strategy. The future belongs to those who take control of their readership, move beyond exclusivity, and build multiple income streams that don't rely on one retailer to survive.

RETAILERS ARE PUSHING MORE ADS

Once upon a time, an author could upload a book to Amazon, optimize their keywords, and—if the book was good enough—let the algorithm do the heavy lifting.

Organic discovery was the lifeblood of indie publishing, allowing well-positioned books to find their audiences without an advertising budget. Those days are quickly disappearing.

Amazon, once a reader-first company, has shifted its focus to advertising revenue, meaning that authors must now pay to be seen. Organic discoverability is being squeezed out by paid placements. Instead of surfacing the best books for readers, Amazon prioritizes books that have an ad budget behind them.

This isn't just happening on Amazon. Apple Books, Kobo, and even Barnes & Noble are increasing their ad offerings, and many of these platforms now prioritize paid listings over organic recommendations. The cost of visibility is going up, and for authors, this means fewer organic sales and more reliance on paid advertising just to maintain the same level of exposure.

But here's the real kicker: advertising costs are rising, but results aren't improving. More authors are bidding on the same ad space, leading to increased competition. The cost per click (CPC) has climbed, meaning authors have to spend more money just to get the same number of eyes on their books. Without a smart strategy, ad costs can quickly outpace revenue, leaving authors burning through their profits in an attempt to keep up.

So, what's the solution? Diversification and ownership. If retailers are making authors pay for visibility, then the smartest move is to build a system where you control your own audience. Instead of depending entirely on Amazon's algorithm to connect with readers, authors need to own their traffic—through direct sales, email lists, and subscription-based platforms like Ream, Patreon, and Substack.

By building an email list, you create a direct line to your readers that doesn't require constant ad spend. Instead of paying Amazon every time you want to reach a new audience, you can email your existing readers for free, turning them into repeat buyers.

By developing a direct sales platform, you reduce your dependence on Amazon's rising ad costs. Selling through your own website means keeping 100% of the sale, rather than losing a cut to Amazon and paying them for the privilege of visibility.

And by expanding into subscription models, you generate predictable, recurring revenue that's not tied to Amazon's changing policies. Platforms like Patreon and Ream allow readers to support their favorite authors directly, giving them early access to new books, exclusive content, and a deeper connection to the creative process.

The bottom line? Retailers will always prioritize their profits over your success. They will keep pushing ad spend higher, squeezing organic discoverability, and making it harder to gain traction without a budget. The authors who thrive in this new landscape will be the ones who diversify, take control of their audience, and stop relying on a single retailer to dictate their future.

SMART PRICING AND MONETIZATION

For years, indie authors have been trained to think in terms of low prices and high volume—the 99-cent book, the permafree series starter, and the Kindle Unlimited page reads. And while those tactics still have their place, the most successful authors today are shifting toward smarter pricing strategies and multiple monetization methods that make each sale more profitable.

One of the biggest game changers in author business is self-liquidating offers through direct sales. Instead of relying solely on retailers, savvy authors are using Shopify, Kickstarter, and other platforms to sell books directly to readers while covering ad costs in the process. Here's how it works: instead of spending money on Amazon or Facebook ads and hoping for a return on a 99-cent ebook, authors are offering bundled deals at a premium price that pays for the ad costs (and then some). This means every dollar spent on ads is immediately recouped, allowing authors to scale their marketing without draining their profits.

Beyond one-time sales, authors are increasingly embracing subscription models to generate predictable, recurring income. Platforms like Substack, Patreon, and Ream allow authors to offer exclusive content, serialized fiction, behind-the-scenes access, or early book releases for a monthly fee. Instead of chasing new readers every month, subscription-based models let authors build a core audience that pays them consistently, reducing reliance on unpredictable book launches.

Another key to maximizing revenue is expanding into multiple formats. While many indie authors focus almost exclusively on ebooks, there's significant money to be made in print-on-demand, audiobooks, and foreign translations. A reader who might hesitate to buy a $4.99 ebook could be happy to pay $19.99 for a paperback or $30 for a signed hardcover edition. Audiobooks, particularly in genres with strong listener demand, create an additional revenue stream that's entirely separate from the crowded ebook market. And with AI-assisted translation services becoming more accessible, offering books in multiple languages can dramatically expand an author's global reach.

The smartest authors today aren't just selling books—they're selling experiences. Limited-edition print runs, exclusive hardcovers, bookplates, and bundled deals give readers a reason to buy direct instead of defaulting to Amazon. And by layering in subscriptions, direct sales, and expanded formats, authors create a business model that isn't dependent on any single platform or pricing strategy.

The bottom line? Authors who rely solely on cheap ebooks and retailer promotions are leaving money on the table. The future belongs to those who think beyond the standard pricing model and create high value offers, multiple revenue streams, and direct connections with their audience.

RUNNING ADS TO A DIRECT STORE VS. RETAILERS: WHY IT'S THE SMARTER LONG-TERM PLAY

For years, authors have been told to run ads directly to their books on Amazon, Apple Books, or Kobo. The logic seemed sound. More traffic meant more visibility, which in turn meant better rankings, which could lead to more organic sales. But over time, as competition increased and retailer ad costs skyrocketed, many authors started to see diminishing returns. Paying for traffic to a retailer was making Amazon richer, not necessarily making authors more profitable.

That's why many successful authors today are shifting their ad spend away from retailers and into direct sales driving traffic to their own Shopify store, Kickstarter page, landing page, or subscription platform rather than sending that hard-earned traffic to Amazon.

When you pay for an ad and send a reader to a retailer, you have zero control over what happens next. Maybe they buy your book, maybe they don't. Maybe they get distracted by other recommendations on the page and buy someone else's book instead. Either way, you've spent money on that click, and the best-case scenario is a single sale where Amazon takes a 30-70% cut.

The problem with this model is that it's a one-time transaction. You don't get the reader's contact information. You can't follow up. You have no way to build a deeper relationship with that customer. If they love your book, they might come back for more—but they also might forget your name entirely, and you'll have to pay for another ad just to remind them you exist.

Now, compare that to what happens when you run an ad to your own store instead of Amazon. A reader clicks on your ad and lands on your Shopify store, where they buy a book directly from you. Not only do you keep 90-95% of the revenue instead of giving Amazon a cut, but now you have something far more valuable than just a sale since you have a customer's email address, purchase history, and a direct line to them for future marketing.

With this information, you can:

- **Follow up with a personal thank-you email**, making them feel appreciated.
- **Offer them an upsell or bundle deal**, increasing their lifetime value immediately.
- **Send them exclusive content, discounts, or early access to new books**, keeping them engaged.
- **Market to them again for free**, without ever paying for another ad to reach them.

This is how a single ad spend turns into long-term profitability. Instead of buying one book and disappearing into Amazon's ecosystem, a reader who buys from you directly becomes part of your world, dramatically increasing the chances that they'll buy from you again.

One of the biggest advantages of running ads to your direct store is the ability to create self-liquidating offers. Instead of simply breaking even (or losing money) on ad spend, you can design bundles, special editions, or higher value offers that immediately cover the cost of acquiring a new customer.

For example, let's say you spend $10 on an ad to acquire a new customer. If you're sending them to Amazon, a single ebook sale might only net you $3-5 in royalties, meaning you're operating at a loss. But if you're selling direct and that reader buys a $30 signed hardcover or a $50 special edition bundle, you've more than covered your ad spend immediately while also gaining a customer you can sell to again.

This is how successful indie authors are scaling their businesses without constantly hemorrhaging ad dollars. They're turning ad spend into an investment, not just an expense because they're not just selling books, they're building an audience they own.

The biggest reason to shift ad spend to direct sales isn't just about making more money per sale. It's about building a sustainable business that isn't controlled by Amazon, Facebook, or any other platform. When you rely entirely on retailers, your success depends on factors you can't control like algorithm changes, policy shifts, ad price fluctuations. But when you build an audience through direct sales, you're in control.

Every reader you acquire through direct sales is a future repeat customer. Every dollar you spend on ads is an investment in your own ecosystem, not someone else's. Over time, this approach compounds, making each launch, each new product, and each marketing campaign more effective.

That's why the smartest authors today aren't just running ads to sell books. They're running ads to build a business. And that's a game-changer.

SUSTAINING GROWTH BEYOND THE LAUNCH

Many authors put all their energy into launching a book, pouring resources into ads, promotions, and retailer algorithms to generate that crucial initial momentum. But once the launch window closes, sales often drop off a cliff. This cycle, filled with intense effort followed by declining returns, leads to burnout, financial instability, and an exhausting sense of starting from scratch with every new release.

The authors who succeed long-term don't just focus on launches, they focus on sustained growth. The key to that growth is diversification. Instead of relying on one platform or one revenue stream, they build a business that continues generating income well beyond the launch phase.

One of the most effective ways to ensure longevity is leveraging multiple revenue streams. Authors who sell directly, expand into audiobooks, offer merchandise, and crowdfund through Kickstarter or Patreon aren't dependent on one income source. When KU payouts drop or ad costs rise, they have other channels supporting their business.

Platforms like Kickstarter and Patreon aren't just for funding special projects anymore, they're viable, recurring income sources that offer stability between launches. A successful Kickstarter campaign can bring in thousands of dollars upfront, covering production costs before a book is even released. Meanwhile, a well-run Patreon or Ream subscription ensures that even during slow months, there's a predictable income stream supporting an author's work.

Another underutilized growth strategy is expanding into international markets. Many indie authors focus only on English-language readers, but there's a massive opportunity in translations. Services like AI-assisted translation tools or working with human translators on a royalty-split model allow authors to tap into new audiences without fronting large costs. Expanding into non-English markets—especially German and French —can extend a book's profitability far beyond its initial launch.

Advertising also plays a role in sustaining growth, but it has to be strategic. The smartest authors don't throw money at ads right after launch, they test and refine their approach first. Using smaller promotional campaigns, they figure out what converts before scaling up ad spend. And they don't start pouring money into ads until they have four or more books in a series, ensuring that every sale has the potential to lead to multiple purchases.

Long-term success isn't about one big launch. It's about creating a system that keeps books selling over time. By diversifying revenue streams, expanding into different formats and markets, and making data-driven ad decisions, authors ensure their business continues to grow without the constant pressure of chasing the next launch.

PLATFORM, AUDIENCE, AND ASSETS

Building a sustainable author career requires aligning three things in a strategic way: *Platform, Audience,* and *Assets.* If you can make these three things work for you, then you'll be on your way to reach your priorities.

- **Platform** refers to the online or offline space where you promote, sell, and engage with your work. It's the foundation for how you share your writing with the world and includes the tools, websites, or systems that allow you to connect with readers and manage your author business.
- **Audience** consists of the people who consume your content, whether that's reading your books, following your blog, engaging with your social media, or subscribing to your newsletter. Understanding your audience is essential because their needs, preferences, and engagement directly impact your success.
- **Assets** are the tools, resources, and intellectual property you already have that can help you grow your author

career. These include everything from your backlist of books, your email list, your social media following, and your unique skills or experiences.

Each of these elements plays a distinct role in how you grow, engage, and monetize your work. When aligned, they create a cohesive system that supports both your creative output and business goals.

PLATFORM: MEETING THE DEMANDS OF THE MARKET

Your platform, whether it's Amazon, Patreon, your website, or social media, has its own unique demands and dynamics. Each one requires a tailored approach to content, engagement, and sales. The key to success is understanding what the platform prioritizes and how you can meet those demands while staying true to your voice and goals.

The main thing I want to get through here is that if a platform isn't helping you grow, then there's no reason to give them your money, time, or attention. So many people are on every platform, even when their incentives are not aligned with, or even in direct opposition with, their goals.

You should only be working on platforms that actively help you grow.

TYPES OF PLATFORMS:

- **Online platforms**: Amazon, Patreon, Substack, your own author website, social media (e.g., Instagram, Twitter, TikTok).

- **Offline platforms**: Bookstore events, speaking engagements, writer conferences, and book signings.

WHAT MAKES A PLATFORM IMPORTANT FOR AUTHORS?

- **Visibility**: Platforms like Amazon or social media provide access to a wide audience, allowing your books or content to be discovered.
- **Sales channels**: Platforms such as your website or eBook stores like Kobo or Amazon are where readers can buy your books directly.
- **Audience engagement**: Platforms like Patreon or a newsletter are where you can build direct, ongoing relationships with your audience, nurturing superfans who support your work long-term.

EXAMPLES:

- **Amazon**: A powerful platform for discoverability, leveraging its algorithm for ranking books and reaching a large, diverse audience.
- **Patreon**: Focuses on community building and deeper, more personal engagement with fans through memberships and exclusive content.

WHAT DOES THE PLATFORM WANT?

Platforms like Amazon are driven by algorithms that favor popular categories, frequent releases, and reader engagement. To thrive here, you need to write to market and optimize your work for the genres or keywords that are currently trending. In contrast, platforms like Patreon may prioritize deeper connections with your audience and regular, smaller updates that foster a sense of community.

On social media, platforms reward engagement and shareable content, like creating bite-sized insights or visuals can help your work go viral.

- **What kind of content does well on the platform:** On Amazon, writing consistent, genre-specific books helps you show up in search results and recommendation algorithms. For Patreon, exclusive behind-the-scenes content, serialized fiction, or fan engagement polls often work best. On social media platforms like Instagram or Twitter, eye-catching visuals or quick, meaningful interactions are vital for expanding your reach.
- **How to align with platform expectations:** To give the platform what it wants, optimize your content. On Amazon, use targeted keywords, book covers that match the expectations of your genre, and release schedules that keep your name in front of readers. On Patreon, offer tiered rewards that reflect your creative process, giving fans a reason to engage at different levels of commitment. On social media, post regularly, engage with your audience, and create content that encourages shares and comments, driving the platform to boost your visibility.

DIFFERENTIATING BETWEEN PLATFORMS

Each platform has different requirements for success. For example:

- **Amazon** requires a focus on keywords, genre conventions, and release frequency.
- **Patreon** is about nurturing community with regular, exclusive content.

- **Social media** is driven by engagement metrics, frequent posts, interactive content, and shareability.

Tailoring your approach to fit the specific platform you're using can maximize your success. Authors often make the mistake of trying to apply the same strategy across platforms, but recognizing and adapting to each platform's demands can dramatically improve your results. I recommend 1-3 platforms, expanding beyond that only when you are established on your previous platforms.

AUDIENCE: ALIGNING YOUR CONTENT WITH READER NEEDS

TYPES OF AUDIENCE:

- **Super fans:** These are the types of people who will fly to meet you or spend $100 on a special edition of their favorite book.
- **Core audience**: Your most loyal readers or superfans who engage with your content regularly, buy your new releases, and advocate for your work.
- **Casual readers**: Readers who may have enjoyed one or two of your books but aren't deeply invested in everything you create.
- **Potential readers**: People who fall within your target demographic but haven't yet discovered your work. These are readers you aim to convert into fans.

WHY UNDERSTANDING YOUR AUDIENCE MATTERS:

- **Targeted content**: Knowing what your audience loves allows you to tailor your work to meet their preferences, increasing the likelihood that they will buy and recommend your books.

- **Engagement**: A clear understanding of your audience helps you build strong relationships through direct engagement, offering them content they're eager to support.
- **Marketing efficiency**: When you know your audience, your marketing becomes more focused and effective. Instead of casting a wide net, you can reach people who are most likely to become loyal readers.

EXAMPLES:

- **Romance readers**: If your audience is primarily romance fans, they may expect certain tropes like happily-ever-afters, and knowing this helps you write and market accordingly.
- **Newsletter subscribers**: These are readers who have given you their contact information and have expressed a deeper interest in your work, making them a valuable group to nurture for long-term success.

Your audience has specific needs, preferences, and pain points. As an author, your success hinges on how well you can align your content with those desires while considering the platform's demands.

WHAT DOES MY AUDIENCE WANT?

Your audience could want different things depending on where they engage with you. For instance, readers on Amazon are often looking for the next book in a series, consistent quality in their favorite genre, or books that fit popular tropes. On social media, your audience may be looking for updates on your writing process, personal engagement, or sneak peeks of upcoming projects.

- **How does this align with the platform's needs?** Your challenge as an author is to align what your audience wants with the platform's mechanisms. If your readers want updates on your writing journey, Patreon is a great platform to offer behind-the-scenes content. If your readers are looking for consistent new releases, Amazon's algorithm will reward you for frequent publishing. On social media, timely posts and interactions keep your readers engaged and can help build buzz for new releases.
- **Creating a feedback loop:** Consistently engaging your audience allows you to understand their changing needs. Use surveys, beta readers, or email list engagement techniques to see what they want and how it aligns with your platform. For instance, if you notice that readers are highly engaged with certain types of updates or book previews, you can double down on those types of content to enhance both audience satisfaction and platform performance.
- **Tailoring for Different Audience Stages:** Newer authors may focus more on building their audience by offering free content or engaging on platforms like Wattpad or social media, where discovery is easier. Established authors, on the other hand, might focus on monetization by launching higher-priced products, exclusive content, or more personalized interactions.

ASSETS: LEVERAGING YOUR UNIQUE STRENGTHS

As an author, you have assets beyond just the words you write. These include your mailing list, social media following, your backlist, or even your personal story. Your assets are the tools that help spur your success and grow your reach beyond your core audience.

WHAT ASSETS DO I HAVE?

Your assets could include:

- **A robust email list**: A direct line to your readers that you own, which allows you to promote new releases, offers, or collaborations without relying on platforms.
- **A backlist of books**: Multiple titles that allow you to leverage different parts of your catalog, bundling books, running sales, or promoting lesser-known works.
- **A strong social media presence**: This is where you can engage fans, run promotions, and drive traffic back to your website or Amazon page.
- **Personal experience or expertise**: If you have unique insights or a niche area of expertise, this can be a powerful asset, especially when building a thought leadership platform or writing non-fiction.

WHY ASSETS ARE CRUCIAL

- **Monetization**: Assets like your backlist or email list can be leveraged to generate income, whether through book sales, memberships, or exclusive content.

- **Growth**: By leveraging your assets strategically, you can expand your reach and increase your visibility across platforms.
- **Audience engagement**: Assets like exclusive content, book bundles, or direct access through email make readers feel more connected to you, which encourages loyalty and repeat purchases.

HOW CAN I LEVERAGE THESE ASSETS TO REACH BEYOND MY CORE AUDIENCE?

To grow beyond your current audience, consider how you can leverage what you already have:

- **Collaborations and partnerships**: Use your network to team up with other authors or influencers in your genre. This can introduce you to new readers while also enhancing your credibility.
- **Cross-promotion**: Utilize your backlist by cross-promoting new releases with older works. For instance, you can offer discounts on previous books when promoting a new release or offer exclusive bundles to your email list.
- **Scaling your brand**: If you have a strong email list or a loyal social media following, consider launching exclusive products, like limited edition signed books, merchandise, or even offering workshops or coaching.

GROWING YOUR ASSETS OVER TIME

Continue nurturing your assets by:

- **Building your email list**: Use lead magnets like free chapters or exclusive short stories.

- **Strengthening your social media**: Be consistent and interactive, offering unique insights that make people want to follow you.
- **Refreshing your backlist**: Update book covers, run promotions, or reformat for new platforms to keep older works generating revenue.

COMMON PITFALLS TO AVOID

Authors often make a few key mistakes when aligning platform, audience, and assets. These include:

- **Neglecting platform demands**: Not optimizing your work for the specific platform, such as failing to use relevant keywords on Amazon or not engaging regularly on social media.
- **Ignoring audience needs**: Focusing too much on what the platform wants without keeping an eye on what your readers are asking for.
- **Underusing assets**: Failing to leverage existing assets like your backlist, email list, or social proof (e.g., reviews and testimonials) to grow your reach.

MEASURABLE ACTION STEPS

To align these three elements, here are some concrete steps you can take:

1. **Platform optimization**: Choose two key platforms and optimize your content (e.g., update keywords on Amazon, increase social media engagement). Track your progress monthly.
2. **Audience feedback loop**: Send out a survey to your email list or social media followers and adjust your content strategy based on the feedback.

3. **Asset leveraging**: Run a promotion using your backlist or cross-promote your new release with older works to boost sales across your catalog.
4. **Growth goals**: Set specific growth targets for each asset, such as increasing your email list by 20% over the next six months or doubling social media engagement through regular posts.

To thrive as an author, you need to think of your platform, audience, and assets as interconnected parts of your overall strategy. Understanding the demands of the platform helps you tailor your content to what will succeed, while knowing your audience ensures that you meet their needs in a way that aligns with the platform's strengths. By leveraging your assets strategically, you can amplify your reach beyond your core audience and build a sustainable author career.

When you align these elements, you create a system where each part supports the others, allowing for growth, engagement, and monetization to happen in a balanced, sustainable way.

AUTHOR SUCCESS PATHS

We've identified five author success paths to help authors build sustainable, thriving careers by focusing on different aspects of their writing and marketing strategies. Each path is a proven way to grow your audience, increase visibility, and drive revenue. Let's explore each of these paths in detail.

VIRALITY / WRITING TO MARKET

Virality refers to content that spreads quickly and organically among readers, often driven by word-of-mouth or social media. Writing to market, on the other hand, means aligning your content with popular trends, tropes, and reader expectations in a specific genre. Both of these strategies focus on maximizing visibility by producing work that resonates widely with readers.

KEY COMPONENTS:

- **Understand reader expectations**: Identify the current trends in your genre by researching bestsellers, reading reviews, and following discussions on forums or social media. For instance, if enemies-to-lovers romance is trending, crafting a novel that fits this trope can increase its appeal.
- **Target high-demand genres**: Writing in popular genres such as romance, thrillers, or sci-fi increases your chances of virality because readers in these markets are actively searching for content that fits their tastes.
- **Optimize for discoverability**: Use relevant keywords, engaging covers, and compelling descriptions to ensure your books stand out on platforms like Amazon or BookBub, where visibility can lead to a viral effect.

ACTIONABLE STEPS FOR AUTHORS:

1. **Market research**: Research trends in your genre and choose a high-demand category to write in.
2. **Align content**: Write to market by using familiar tropes and delivering the story beats that readers expect, but with your own unique spin to stand out.

3. **Encourage sharing**: Include features in your book or marketing strategy that make it easy to share, like social media-ready quotes or special editions that encourage fans to spread the word.

In our Author Ecosystem framework, we call these Deserts.

Deserts are pliable creators who are good at writing to market and audience. They can make unemotional business decisions and can also ride a trend by delivering a solid experience. When they find a trend they want to ride, they are usually very good at hitting the market at the right time and place. They also do a good job of doubling down on things that seem to be working, and tend to put all their chips on one square.

Because Deserts are good at riding trends, they need to have a few different skill sets, including strong research skills, ability to produce quickly, and willingness to detach, both to double down on what's working well, and to cut activity on anything that's not working. Deserts tend to put all their sustenance in one cactus and build a highly profitable pathway of readers to sales. This brings more money in the short term, though it can put their business at risk if any aspect of their system dries up. Many Deserts balance this risk by having multiple pen names or by maintaining a freelance career on the side that they can always fall back on.

Healthy Deserts maintain a camel hump (or several) where they can store away their "riches in the niches" to get them between oases where water is plentiful. They watch the warning signs that the market is changing, and they pivot when necessary—to another genre, to another source of readers, or to another platform. Unhealthy Deserts stray too far from a water source and end up thirsty when one or several of their money makers dries up. Because this type is focused more in the short-term, it's extremely important that they feel confident in their ability to figure it out, though in their unhealthy versions, they fly too close to the sun.

CONTENT MARKETING / THOUGHT LEADERSHIP

Content marketing involves consistently producing valuable content that attracts and engages your target audience. Thought leadership takes this a step further by establishing you as an authority in your niche, building trust with your audience, and positioning you as a go-to resource.

KEY COMPONENTS:

- **Write for your readers**: Focus on delivering content that solves a problem or provides valuable insights. This could be in the form of blog posts, newsletters, or videos. For non-fiction authors, this is especially critical, but even fiction authors can build thought leadership by discussing writing craft, industry trends, or the themes in their books.
- **Engage consistently**: Whether through your blog, social media, or newsletter, build a steady stream of content that keeps you top of mind for your audience.
- **Establish authority**: Use guest posts, podcast interviews, or articles to share your insights and experiences with a wider audience. By consistently delivering valuable content, you establish yourself as a thought leader in your niche.

ACTIONABLE STEPS FOR AUTHORS:

1. **Content strategy**: Develop a plan for producing blog posts, podcasts, or newsletters that speak directly to your audience's needs.
2. **Authority building**: Contribute guest content to other platforms to expand your reach and establish yourself as a credible expert in your field.
3. **Community engagement**: Respond to comments, ask for feedback, and create content that sparks discussion and engagement, helping you build stronger relationships with your audience.

In our Author Ecosystem framework, we call these Grasslands.

Grasslands are focused, deep delvers that seek out popular topics that align to their interests. They plant grass to feel out a plain, but when they find something that takes root with a large potential audience, they quickly go extremely deep with it, deeper than anyone else has the energy to do! They tend to consider every angle of their genre, niche, or topic, so when they put something out, it tends to blow people's minds and rise to the top. In nonfiction, they tend to be correct about whatever their thesis is. Grasslands are capable of becoming the absolute best-in-class at whatever they do, which is why they need to choose new potential projects carefully!

Because Grasslands are intense and obsessive about their chosen topic, they must stay focused to see the fruits of it. It does not serve them well to have multiple projects going at once because they don't have the energy to devote to each one. It also doesn't typically work for them to cross over audiences between two different interests, unlike some of the other types.

Healthy Grasslands find fertile soil to take root in and grow the tallest, most epic tree in the garden. They also dedicate so much of their energy to one area that they become above reproach. Unhealthy Grasslands plant a lot of seeds but never gain momentum in any one area, and struggle to deliver on deadlines they've set for themselves.

LAUNCH CYCLES

A well-executed launch cycle can make or break the success of a new book. This path involves planning your book launches strategically to maximize sales and visibility during the critical launch period and sustain momentum afterward.

KEY COMPONENTS:

- **Pre-launch planning**: Build anticipation for your book well before its release. This can involve cover reveals, sneak peeks, ARC (Advance Reader Copy) distribution, and pre-order campaigns.
- **Release strategy**: Launch events, special promotions, and partnerships with bloggers or influencers can help generate excitement and ensure that your book gets noticed.
- **Post-launch momentum**: After the initial release, continue to promote the book through advertising, guest appearances, and continued engagement with readers.

ACTIONABLE STEPS FOR AUTHORS:

1. **Pre-launch timeline**: Create a timeline for each launch phase (3–6 months before the release) and assign

specific tasks like cover reveals, pre-orders, and reader engagement.
2. **Leverage influencers**: Build relationships with bloggers, podcasters, and reviewers to get your book in front of new audiences.
3. **Sustaining sales**: After the launch, maintain momentum through promotional campaigns, cross-promotions with other authors, and ongoing audience engagement.

These people utilize the build, launch, recover cycle. In our Author Ecosystem framework, we call these Tundras.

Tundras love to build cool things and launch them, and they are extremely well-versed in turning a ton of attention to themselves and their project for a short period of time. They are the type to study the platform and see what trends they can tap into to make their next launch bigger, and they are most likely to know how they are going to market and sell something before creating it. Once done with a project, they wipe their hands free of it and rarely think much of it again now that the launch is over!

Because Tundras survive on a feast and famine cycle, they need to be able to peel as much meat from the bone as possible. Tundras become stackers: stackers of trend, stackers of value, stackers of audience. They are comfortable with having a lot of one-off projects and comfortable with building a diverse audience that only likes a portion of their catalog, though they welcome superfans who enjoy everything, too!

Healthy Tundras have a firm understanding of their seasons and build safeguards to make sure there's never a point of starvation. They also learn to connect their body of work, usually somewhat disparate projects, under one banner so that every launch offers a bigger feast on their backlist. Unhealthy Tundras struggle to create enough feast to get through the famine periods, leaving them burnt out and under-resourced before the next launch.

AMBASSADOR MARKETING / COMMUNITY BUILDING

Ambassador marketing involves turning your most loyal readers into advocates who help spread the word about your books. Community building focuses on cultivating a dedicated fanbase that actively supports your work and feels personally connected to your journey as an author.

KEY COMPONENTS:

- **Identify ambassadors**: Your superfans can be your biggest asset in marketing your books. These readers will often volunteer to share your work, leave reviews, or even promote your books on social media.
- **Foster community**: Build spaces (Facebook groups, Patreon communities, Discord channels) where your readers can engage with each other and with you. By creating these spaces, you build a sense of belonging, turning casual readers into lifelong fans.
- **Reward loyalty**: Give ambassadors exclusive content, early access to new releases, or special shout-outs. This strengthens their connection to you and motivates them to continue spreading the word.

ACTIONABLE STEPS FOR AUTHORS:

1. **Superfan engagement**: Create a group or community where your most engaged readers can connect with you directly. Offer special perks like early access or exclusive content to incentivize deeper engagement.

2. **Incentivize ambassadors**: Encourage your readers to share your work by creating referral programs or offering rewards for their advocacy.
3. **Nurture relationships**: Regularly check in with your ambassadors, involve them in your creative process, and make them feel like a valued part of your author journey.

In our Author Ecosystems framework, we call these Forests.

Forests are often marching to the beat of their interests and putting their own unique spin on everything they do for their readers. They have a close relationship with their fans largely because they inject so much of their own personality into all their books. They could write a murder mystery, a sweet romance, and cozy comedy, and readers will gobble it up because it's [insert name here]'s take on the genre!

Because Forests are multi-passionate, they tend to have multiple pen names going at once. Whereas this might overwhelm other types, Forests are good at watering each of their trees every year on a consistent schedule so everything grows steadily. They are extremely competent and tend to stack an impressive number of skills to deliver high-quality work across everything they do. Forests are good at being top of the class and being part of the conversation. To do this, Forests must be consistent, hardworking, and patient, as it takes time, energy, and money to stand up each of their trees. (And they still need to do so one at a time to get a bit of momentum in one area before moving on to another!)

Healthy Forests survive by cross-pollinating their work across all their interests. The key connection is their personality, and their fans gravitate toward them for *who they are* rather than what they do or write. Unhealthy Forests chase trends, explore too many interests at once, and don't pay close enough attention to the marketplace to ensure enough others will share their interests.

STRATEGIC PARTNERSHIPS

Partnerships with other authors, influencers, or organizations can amplify your reach and create opportunities for mutual growth. This strategy is about leveraging the networks of others to extend your visibility and credibility.

KEY COMPONENTS:

- **Collaborate with authors**: Whether through co-writing projects, shared marketing initiatives, or group anthologies, teaming up with other authors in your genre can open you up to their readers and expand your reach.
- **Cross-promotions**: Partner with other creators, such as podcasters, bloggers, or YouTubers, to cross-promote your work. This helps you tap into new audiences that may not have discovered you yet.
- **Joint events**: Hosting webinars, live chats, or virtual book tours with other authors or experts can increase engagement and attract attention from a larger audience.

ACTIONABLE STEPS FOR AUTHORS:

1. **Identify potential partners**: Look for authors or influencers in your genre or niche who share your values or target audience.
2. **Plan collaborative projects**: Work together on anthologies, book bundles, or cross-promotions to reach new readers.
3. **Leverage shared networks**: Use your partner's platform (and vice versa) to promote your joint venture, ensuring that both parties gain new followers and increased visibility.

In our Author Ecosystems framework, we call these Aquatics.

Aquatics are excited about everything and want to create an immersive experience for their readers. They know exactly what their fans want and this dictates both what they create and how they market. If their fans won't follow them to this or that platform, they don't go there! If their fans want to see their bestselling novel as a comic book, they create it for them, even if they have no idea how to make a comic book. (They'll learn!)

Because Aquatics build their business horizontally and have their hands in many different formats as well as merchandise, they must be competent at many skill sets, like building large stories and worlds, delegating, building a functional team that understands the bigger vision, maintaining a strong connection to fans, and expanding slowly and as time, energy, money, and other resources allow.

Healthy Aquatics survive by creating cool new things that both service their current audience and help them grow a larger audience. Unhealthy Aquatics create too many things with disparate audiences, spreading themselves too thin and losing momentum across everything.

Each of these paths offers a different route to success, and most authors will benefit from a combination of these strategies. Whether you're focusing on writing to market for virality, building thought leadership through content marketing, or cultivating a loyal community through ambassador marketing, the key is to align your approach with your goals, audience, and assets. Understanding these paths helps you structure your career for sustainable growth and long-term success.

The questions you should ask here are

- What ecosystem/strategy feels the best to me right now?
- Where do my natural strengths lie?

MEDIA CHANNELS

Amplification strategies evolve as your career progresses. as you grow your ***owned, earned, paid,*** and ***borrowed*** media channels. I wrote about these a lot in this article, but here's a little summary of all four channels.

OWNED MEDIA

Owned media refers to the platforms and content that you have complete control over. These are the channels that you directly manage and where you can consistently communicate your message without relying on external parties. Owned media is essential for establishing your brand, building a loyal audience, and creating a hub where people can regularly engage with your work.

EXAMPLES OF OWNED MEDIA CHANNELS:

- **Website/Blog:** Your personal website or blog is a central hub for your content, including articles, updates, resources, and other information about your work. It's a primary space where you control the user experience and the messaging.

- **Email newsletter:** Newsletters allow you to communicate directly with your audience, providing regular updates, exclusive content, and personal insights. Since you own your email list, it's a reliable way to reach your audience without depending on external algorithms.

- **Social media profiles:** While social media platforms themselves are not owned, the profiles and pages you maintain on platforms like Twitter, Instagram, LinkedIn, and Facebook are spaces where you control the content and how often you post.

- **Podcasts and YouTube channels:** If you create and manage your own podcast or YouTube channel, these serve as owned media where you have complete control over the topics, format, and audience interaction.

- **Books and ebooks:** Your published works, whether traditional or self-published, are forms of owned media that reflect your voice, brand, and expertise.

- **Online courses or membership sites:** Platforms where you host your own content, such as online courses or member communities, provide a controlled environment to deliver value and engage deeply with your audience.

EARNED MEDIA

Earned media refers to the exposure you gain through organic, unpaid methods. Essentially, it's the recognition you "earn" rather than pay for. This includes any media coverage, word-of-mouth, social media mentions, shares, reviews, and any other form of promotion that comes from outside your direct control. It's often seen as one of the most credible forms of media because it's driven by others talking about your work rather than by your own marketing efforts.

EXAMPLES OF EARNED MEDIA CHANNELS:

- **Press coverage:** Articles, interviews, or mentions in news outlets, blogs, or industry publications.
- **Social media mentions:** Shares, likes, comments, or posts by others on platforms like Twitter, Facebook, LinkedIn, or Instagram.
- **Reviews and testimonials:** Reviews on platforms like Goodreads, Amazon, or endorsements from readers and other authors.
- **Word-of-mouth:** Personal recommendations from readers, peers, or influencers.
- **User-generated content:** Content created by your audience, such as fan art, videos, or blogs related to your work.

BORROWED MEDIA

Borrowed media, sometimes referred to as "shared media," involves leveraging someone else's platform to reach their audience. This type of media includes guest appearances, collaborations, or content that is published on platforms or channels not owned by you but where you have permission to share your message. The key here is that you're using someone else's established audience to amplify your voice, often through partnerships or mutual agreements.

EXAMPLES OF BORROWED MEDIA CHANNELS:

- **Guest blog posts:** Writing for other websites, blogs, or newsletters that have a built-in audience interested in your niche.
- **Podcast appearances:** Being a guest on podcasts to share your insights, which helps reach new listeners.
- **Social media takeovers:** Temporarily taking over someone else's social media account to interact with their followers.
- **Collaborative content:** Joint webinars, articles, or videos where you work with other creators to reach both of your audiences.
- **Influencer collaborations:** Working with influencers who share your content or discuss your work on their platforms.

PAID MEDIA

Paid media involves any form of advertising or promotional content that you pay for to reach a broader audience. This includes ads on social media, search engines, display ads, paid influencers, sponsored posts, and more. Paid media is an effective way to quickly increase visibility, drive traffic, and boost engagement, especially when you're looking to reach specific demographics or expand beyond your existing audience.

EXAMPLES OF PAID MEDIA CHANNELS:

- **Social media ads:** Paid ads on platforms like Facebook, Instagram, Twitter, LinkedIn, and TikTok allow you to target specific audiences based on demographics, interests, and behaviors.

- **Search engine advertising:** Pay-per-click (PPC) ads on search engines like Google and Bing help you appear at the top of search results for relevant keywords, driving traffic to your website or landing pages.
- **Display ads:** Banner ads on websites, blogs, or apps that reach audiences as they browse other content online. These can be targeted based on user interests, site content, or retargeting past visitors.
- **Influencer marketing:** Paying influencers to promote your content, product, or service on their platforms, leveraging their audience to gain visibility and credibility.
- **Sponsored content:** Paying for articles, videos, or posts that appear on media outlets, blogs, or social platforms to promote your message in a way that blends with the editorial content.

As your career grows, you will have success in all of these, but which one are you going to focus on right now?

OTHER MARKETING STRATEGIES

In a world where new releases hit virtual shelves every day, simply having a book on the market is no longer enough. Authors must stand out, not just once at launch, but continually, in order to stay on readers' radars. While the basics, like announcing a new release on social media or running a small ad campaign, may provide a temporary boost, true longevity comes from strategic, multifaceted marketing.

This chapter focuses on the techniques that go beyond surface-level tactics, diving into the realm of advanced email funnels, collaborative efforts like anthologies, and targeted influencer promotions. It also explores the power of affiliate partnerships and the credibility that well-placed media appearances can bring. By weaving together these tools, authors create a steady current of reader engagement, transforming one-time browsers into loyal fans who eagerly await every new book. Think of it as assembling a suite of instruments that, when played in harmony, make your author brand impossible to ignore.

PROMO STACKING: LAYERING MULTIPLE PROMOTIONS FOR EXPONENTIAL EFFECT

In today's crowded book market, relying on a single promotional tool often isn't enough to make a meaningful dent in visibility. That's where promo stacking comes in. Rather than rolling out different promotions haphazardly, you plan and execute them in quick succession (or with strategic overlap) so that each effort builds on the momentum of the last. It's a bit like orchestrating a series of fireworks: individually, each can be striking, but when they happen in a coordinated display, they create a far more memorable spectacle.

One common approach to promo stacking starts with scheduling multiple newsletter promotions from various reader-curation services. Platforms like BookBub, Freebooksy, Bargain Booksy, and others each have their own loyal followings who trust their recommendations. By booking spots with several services over the course of a few days or a week, you create multiple spikes in visibility and sales. This can help your book climb retailer rankings repeatedly, rather than just once, maintaining high visibility for a longer stretch.

To amplify these newsletter ads, authors layer on Facebook or Amazon Ads. While a newsletter feature can deliver an instant surge of traffic, the impact can fade quickly if it's not sustained. Targeted ads on Facebook and Amazon extend that window of momentum, ensuring you're still reaching new readers even after the initial newsletter-driven surge subsides. If you coordinate the timing, you'll effectively funnel that newsletter audience into your ad retargeting cycle, turning quick bursts of attention into a steady stream of sales or downloads.

The real beauty of promo stacking lies in how it triggers recommendation algorithms on retailer platforms. Multiple sales spikes in a short time frame can push a book into higher-ranking categories or earn it a spot on bestseller or "hot new releases" lists. Once these algorithms latch on, your book gains additional organic exposure, showing up in "also-bought" sections or as a recommended title for people who've purchased similar reads. This extra visibility can linger for days or even weeks, offering a substantial return on the upfront cost of the promotions.

However, the key to successful promo stacking is tight coordination and careful budgeting. Mapping out your calendar in advance and knowing exactly which newsletters are going out on which days and how your ad spend will be allocated prevents you from spreading your resources too thin. It also allows you to track which parts of the stack deliver the strongest results. Did the bulk of your sales come from a specific newsletter, or did Facebook Ads drive more conversions than Amazon Ads? Gathering these insights helps you optimize future campaigns, trimming what doesn't work, and doubling down on what does.

Ultimately, promo stacking isn't just about making a splash; it's about creating a rolling wave of visibility that sweeps across multiple channels. By overlapping different promotions in a short window, you multiply each tactic's impact, providing a much stronger push than you'd get by spacing them out. And once you've orchestrated a successful stack, you'll have a blueprint for repeating— perhaps even improving—the process for future releases.

ATTENTION DOMINATION: MAXIMIZING IMPACT WITH LIMITED RESOURCES

When budgets are tight, one of the most effective strategies is an intensive, short-term push often referred to as "attention domination." The idea is simple but powerful: by orchestrating numerous promotional activities over a condensed period, you create the impression that your book is suddenly everywhere. Readers encounter it multiple times in different ways. Perhaps they see an interview on a podcast, a social media post by a trusted influencer, and a retargeting ad all within the same week. Because people typically need several touchpoints before making a purchase, clustering these touchpoints together accelerates their decision-making process and increases the likelihood that they'll pick up your book.

Attention domination works especially well for authors operating on smaller budgets, as it leverages timing and repetition rather than relying on expensive ad campaigns that run for weeks or months. The trick is to coordinate carefully. Align your email announcements, social media reveals, influencer shoutouts, and any paid ads to go live at roughly the same time and work with reliable vendors who will deliver on time. If you have a small ad budget, aim for a narrow window—two to seven days—where your book's visibility peaks. This concentration ensures that even a modest investment feels overwhelming to readers in a specific niche.

Like above, a key advantage of this approach is the way it can also trigger algorithms on retailer sites. A spike in sales or downloads over a short period can boost your ranking, which in turn exposes the book to even more potential readers who browse bestseller lists or "also-bought" recommendations. Once that happens, the retailer's own system helps sustain momentum without additional spending, effectively turning your short-term push into a longer-lasting wave of visibility.

Measuring the impact of an attention-domination campaign requires a holistic view. Individual metrics like clicks, opens, or short-term sales matter, but the real question is whether your overall strategy significantly elevated the book's profile in your target market. Did you see a noticeable jump in online reviews or social media mentions? Did your email list grow, or did organic traffic to your website increase? By looking at these broader indicators, you can gauge whether your sprint approach truly captured and held readers' attention.

Ultimately, attention domination is a high-impact, low-duration tactic that pairs well with the longer, more sustained strategies outlined elsewhere. It's not meant to replace consistent engagement and relationship-building, but rather to amplify it—offering a jolt of energy that can catapult a launch or a sales push to new heights, even when funds are limited.

COLLABORATION & ANTHOLOGIES: JOINING FORCES FOR BIGGER REACH

In the ever-evolving landscape of book marketing, collaboration has become one of the most effective ways for authors to expand their audience and sustain visibility. Instead of operating in isolation, successful authors strategically align themselves with peers, leveraging shared audiences and collective marketing power. The key to this approach lies in partnerships, especially through cross-promotions, anthologies, and multi-author collaborations that amplify reach without requiring massive ad spend.

Anthologies, in particular, offer a unique way to pool readership and create lasting engagement. When multiple authors contribute to a single collection, they bring their individual audiences into a shared ecosystem. Readers who buy an anthology to support one of their favorite authors are introduced to others in the same genre, leading to organic growth and cross-pollination of fan bases. These collaborations work best when structured around a unifying theme or niche, ensuring that all contributors appeal to a similar demographic. Anthologies can be launched strategically, aligning with major book events, promotions, or seasonal themes to maximize visibility.

Beyond anthologies, co-writing and series crossovers are another high-impact collaboration strategy. When two or more authors team up to write interconnected stories, they build an extended universe that incentivizes readers to explore more of their work. For instance, authors in a shared genre can create companion novellas that link their characters, worlds, or overarching plots. This approach not only drives additional sales but also fosters a deeper emotional connection between readers and the author community.

Newsletter swaps and cross-promotions also play a crucial role in expanding an author's reach. By featuring each other's books in their respective newsletters, authors introduce their readers to similar works in a trusted, personal way. Unlike cold advertising, these promotions come with built-in credibility, increasing the likelihood that readers will engage and buy.

Joint promotional events, such as multi-author giveaways, live panels, and virtual book tours, add another layer of exposure. Whether hosted on social media, in private reader groups, or as part of a larger book fair, these events generate excitement and drive engagement across multiple platforms.

Ultimately, collaboration isn't just about visibility, it's about community. Readers enjoy discovering new authors through trusted recommendations, and when authors support each other, they build a sustainable network that benefits everyone involved. By tapping into anthologies, shared series, newsletter swaps, and joint promotions, authors create a ripple effect that extends far beyond what they could achieve alone.

INFLUENCER MARKETING

Influencer marketing has become an increasingly pivotal tool for authors looking to amplify their reach in a crowded online landscape. The concept is simple yet powerful. Rather than trying to speak to the world all by yourself, you tap into the passionate, engaged audiences that already gather around personalities on platforms like Instagram, TikTok, YouTube, and beyond. What sets influencer marketing apart from other promotional tactics is the trust factor. When readers see someone they already follow, respect, or admire sharing a book recommendation, they're far more likely to pay attention than if they spot a conventional ad scrolling through their feed.

A successful influencer campaign begins with genuine alignment. Authors often make the mistake of approaching influencers purely based on their follower counts, but it's actually relevance and authenticity that move the needle. A micro-influencer who regularly features book reviews within your genre can yield better results than a mega-celebrity whose content has nothing to do with reading. By reaching out to influencers who have cultivated communities that match your target audience, you ensure that your book doesn't feel like a random product placement, it becomes a natural extension of the influencer's brand.

The most fruitful relationships with influencers often evolve into long-term collaborations, rather than one-off promotions. Sending advanced reader copies or inviting influencers to exclusive cover reveals fosters a sense of partnership. When they feel invested in the book's journey, their enthusiasm translates into organic content like unboxing videos, reading vlogs, or spontaneous social media shoutouts. This approach also allows the influencer's audience to see your book multiple times in varying contexts, gradually building a sense of familiarity and anticipation.

Beyond creating immediate buzz, influencer marketing lays the groundwork for sustained word-of-mouth. People trust recommendations from figures they've come to know online, and that trust extends beyond a single post or story. By actively engaging with influencer-generated content— thanking them, resharing their reviews, or even appearing for live Q&A sessions—you forge a deeper connection with both the influencer and their followers. Over time, these readers become part of your broader community, eager for future releases and updates. In a digital environment awash with quick-hit ads, this kind of authentic, influencer-led engagement stands out, providing a valuable bridge between your work and the readers who are most likely to love it.

AFTERWORD

When we started *The Six Figure Author Experiment*, we didn't know exactly where it would take us. What began as an experiment in direct sales, Kickstarter, and author sustainability evolved into a framework for a thriving, independent publishing business. This book is the culmination of that journey, pulling together years of conversations, data, and hands-on experience into a cohesive strategy.

The path to success isn't a straight line. It's an ongoing process of testing, refining, and learning from real-world results. We've seen firsthand how authors can go from uncertain about their next steps to completely transforming their businesses, not through luck, but by layering proven strategies that work together as a system.

At first, it might feel overwhelming. You might be asking: *Where do I start? How do I apply all of this without burning out?* The answer is simple: Start with one piece and make it work.

If you're launching a book, try running a Kickstarter instead of a traditional retailer launch. If you've already done that, optimize your post-campaign funnel to move backers into your direct sales ecosystem. If you're selling direct but struggling with conversions, refine your landing pages and test new offers. Each step builds on the last, making every future launch stronger and easier.

This approach isn't about chasing one big breakthrough. It's about building momentum launch by launch, campaign by campaign until direct sales aren't just an experiment, but the foundation of a profitable, sustainable author business.

By this point, you've seen the full scope of what it means to build a thriving direct sales business as an author. The strategies in this book aren't just theories, they are the real-world-tested results of countless experiments, both from our own businesses and from the authors we've studied, collaborated with, and learned from.

But knowledge alone isn't enough.

One of the biggest challenges we see authors face isn't a lack of ideas; it's the overwhelming number of possibilities. Once you see the potential of Kickstarter, direct sales, web stores, and reader subscriptions, the question isn't "Can this work?" It's "Where do I even start?"

If there's one lesson we hope sticks with you, it's this: *you don't have to do everything at once.*

Most six-figure direct sales authors didn't build their businesses overnight. They started small, tested what worked, and then layered in new strategies over time. They didn't launch a web store, a Kickstarter, a subscription, and an entire ecosystem all at once. They began with one clear step and built from there.

This is a process of iteration. The first time you set up a direct sales store, it won't be perfect. The first time you run a Kickstarter, you'll learn things that will improve the next one. Every campaign, every launch, every marketing effort gives you data to refine and improve. Success isn't about having the perfect plan; it's about taking consistent action and adapting as you go.

And here's the truth that often gets buried under all the tactics: this work is creative.

Too often, authors separate business from art, thinking of sales and marketing as something separate from writing. But building a direct sales system isn't just about making money. It's about crafting an experience for your readers. It's about designing a world that they want to step into, a journey that they want to take with you.

Whether it's the anticipation of a Kickstarter launch, the excitement of a special edition, or the connection of an engaged community, every part of this system is an extension of your creative work. The authors who thrive in direct sales aren't just skilled at business—they treat their sales process with the same level of craft as their books.

So, as you step forward, don't feel pressured to do everything immediately. Choose one piece that resonates with you, implement it, and build from there. The key to long-term success isn't speed, it's sustainability.

What you've built so far in your career has gotten you to this point. What you build next will determine where you go from here. The difference between authors who stay stuck and those who thrive isn't knowledge, it's execution.

The next step is yours.

If you loved this book, I hope you go check out *The Author Stack,* my weekly newsletter that goes into even more depth about how to build your creator career.

https://www.theauthorstack.com/

As a paid member, you get access to a ton of my previous work, including fiction, non-fiction, courses, and more.

RESOURCES:

- *How to Build Your Creative Career*
- *How to Become a Successful Author*
- *Advanced Growth Tactics for Authors*
- Create Profitable Facebook Ads course
- Fund Your Book with Kickstarter course
- How to set up and run an awesome anthology course
- How to run a viral giveaway to build your mailing list
- Write a Great Novel course
- How to Build an Audience from Scratch minicourse
- 10x your productivity course
- Complete Creative data archive
- Income reports since 2018
- Script library

There's probably even more now since I update it every couple of months.

You can also find my work at: www.russellnohelty.com

Feel free to email me at russell@wannabepress.com and let me know what you think, and please leave a review. The only way I know I should keep writing these kinds of books is from your reviews and kind words.

Find more of my work at my blog:

www.theauthorstack.com

Find all my work at my website:

www.russellnohelty.com

Bookbub:

https://www.bookbub.com/profile/russell-nohelty